Make it Lighter

Angela Nilsen

Make it Lighter

Healthier versions of your favourite recipes
All the taste – none of the guilt

Angela Nilsen

hamlyn

An Hachette UK Company
www.hachette.co.uk

First published in Great Britain in 2014 by Hamlyn,
a division of Octopus Publishing Group Ltd
Endeavour House
189 Shaftesbury Avenue
London
WC2H 8JY
www.octopusbooks.co.uk

ISBN 978-0-600-62772-2

A CIP catalogue record for this book is available from the British Library

Printed and bound in China

10 9 8 7 6 5 4 3 2 1

Both metric and imperial measurements are given for the recipes.
Use one set of measures only, not a mixture of both.

Standard level spoon measurements are used in all recipes
1 tablespoon = 15 ml
1 teaspoon = 5 ml

Ovens should be preheated to the specified temperature. If using a fan-assisted oven, follow the manufacturer's instructions for adjusting the time and temperature. Grills should also be preheated.

This book includes dishes made with nuts and nut derivatives. It is advisable for those with known allergic reactions to nuts and nut derivatives and those who may be potentially vulnerable to these allergies, such as pregnant and nursing mothers, invalids, the elderly, babies and children, to avoid dishes made with nuts and nut oils. It is also prudent to check the labels of preprepared ingredients for the possible inclusion of nut derivatives. The Department of Health advises that eggs should not be consumed raw. This book contains some dishes made with raw or lightly cooked eggs. It is prudent for more vulnerable people such as pregnant and nursing mothers, invalids, the elderly, babies and young children to avoid uncooked or lightly cooked dishes made with eggs.

Contents

Introduction

I'd like to introduce you to this book by saying as loudly as I can, 'this is not a diet book'. Dieting can so easily equate with deprivation and that is not what the recipes within these pages are about. Instead, the intention is to offer simple, achievable and practical ideas that will help you eat in a healthy, balanced way, without feeling cheated.

Healthy but nice

The idea for 'Make it Lighter' came from a regular feature I had been commissioned to write for *BBC Good Food Magazine*, called 'Make it Healthier'. The brief was to suggest a recipe makeover each month for readers' favourite 'naughty but nice' recipes – potato Dauphinoise or lemon drizzle cake, for example – to provide 'healthy but nice' alternatives. You'll find no surprises in the recipe titles – they are all classics, the kinds of food you love to eat but might feel a bit guilty about. My challenge was to find ways of maintaining the desired taste while creating a much lighter version: recipes with less fat, sugar or salt – the very ingredients that make them so popular in the first place.

It has not always been easy, as my starting point for each recipe was that there should be no compromise on the irresistible rich taste or look that you would expect from the original. Furthermore, I wasn't interested in using lots of 'light' alternatives to full-fat ingredients, since for me they don't offer the same taste experience. Where I have occasionally used them, I've worked out lower-fat ways of increasing richness and flavour.

After creating a number of these recipes for the magazine, and with current trends for eating more healthily, it seemed timely to put the collection into a book. To expand the idea further, and make the book even more useful – whether you are looking for family supper ideas, lighter ways to entertain or guilt-free baking – I have added lots of new recipes, such as coffee panna cotta, fish cakes and sticky gingerbread.

Challenging work

Working out how to come up with a lighter version of a recipe that relies heavily on fat, salt or sugar for its taste, texture and appearance can be daunting and I've often begun the process by wondering how on earth it can be done. How can cookies be crisp and buttery and yet keep fat and sugar to a minimum? However, I always manage to find a way and am invariably surprised by how good the results can be when fat, sugar and salt are removed or reduced.

But it's not all about taking away and reducing. There's also an element of working out what I need to replace ingredients with or add to a recipe to keep it tempting. Sometimes a trick ingredient can turn a recipe around. While struggling with the recipe for chocolate brownies, I remembered a cake I used to make while living in Canada that was made with mayonnaise instead of butter. On adapting this idea, a high-fat treat became deceptively lighter. A friend mentioned that her latest way of making hummus used a whole bulb of roasted garlic and very little else, so when creating the hummus recipe for this book I experimented with this idea and found it solved the problem of providing flavour and creaminess without having to mix in too much oil and tahini.

With other recipes success lies more in adapting how they are made. For each one I work out new ways to cook, mix or handle it that will maintain the desired characteristics. Altering the cooking technique, for example, can often instantly lower the fat. Instead of frying vegetables in lots of oil, just brush them with a minimum amount and roast or griddle them instead. You will find similar healthy cooking tips within each recipe, providing all sorts of ideas that can be used again and again, whatever you are cooking, to help you cook more healthily.

Nutrition know-how

After researching each recipe and before testing begins, I speak with a nutritionist to find out its main dangers and toss ideas around about ingredient options: what would be best to go or be reduced and what might be included in its place to make it more healthy? My shepherd's pie was transformed to a super-healthy version when nutritionist Fiona Hunter suggested substituting some of the mince for lentils. 'You'll never guess they are in there,' she told me – and no one did. For fish chowder, salt and fat levels were dramatically reduced when nutritionist Kerry Torrens suggested switching lardons for prosciutto. I also dip into my own fat-busting skills and recall tips I have gathered from chefs and other food writers I've worked with over the years, or make use of techniques and ideas I have discovered myself along the way.

All the recipes in this book have been tested, often several times, in order to make adjustments until the ultimate lighter version has been achieved. Things can go wrong during testing, but a disaster can throw up surprising new ways to make a dish even better. Baking recipes can be especially tricky, as it is the fat and sugar that keep them light and moist. My first attempt at banana bread didn't rise and was incredibly stodgy. I'd eliminated too much. But having it go wrong helped me to work out how to put it right and the second attempt rose beautifully.

Sweet temptations

Of course, there have been times when I've thought a dish just isn't meant to be healthy, like lemon tart. But the more recipes I lighten up – and the more ways I find to do it – the more I find I prefer my versions to the much richer alternatives. My palette has adjusted to expecting less fat, salt and sugar. This doesn't mean I don't enjoy the occasional higher-fat or sweet treat, but such dishes are not the focus of my diet.

It is important not to put more calories into our bodies than we are able to use up in energy. So to make the most of these lighter recipes, do use them as part of an ongoing, healthy, balanced diet. That means eating a range of foods from the main food groups – fruit and vegetables (a variety of at least five portions a day is recommended), milk and dairy, meat, fish, eggs and pulses, and starchy foods like bread, pasta, rice and potatoes – and choosing only small quantities of ones with fat and sugar. Cutting down on salt is also advisable (for adults the recommendation is no more than 6 g a day). If you taste before you season, especially when cooking with salty ingredients like stock, anchovies or Parmesan cheese, chances are that you will need to add very little extra salt, if any at all.

Charted data

Nutritional therapist Kerry Torrens has been a hugely supportive advisor while writing this book. She contributed to initial discussions for each recipe as well as while making them, as I deliberated over which ingredients to use in order to make each recipe as healthy as it can be. She has also created charts that compare the classic version per serving with the lighter one. In addition, easily recognizable symbols highlight other nutritional aspects. For more information, turn to page 10.

You be the judge

Although I have given careful consideration to the healthiness of each recipe, it is important to me not to compromise the taste simply to improve its healthy attributes even further. Before I decide if I'm happy with the final version, I ask myself 'but does it taste good, would I make it again?' If the answer is 'no', it may mean a bit more fat or sugar has to be reintroduced, or something else is tweaked, until the answer is 'yes'. But it's when one of my tasters says they can't tell the difference between the lighter and the classic version that I know I'm on to a winner. I hope that many of the recipes in this book will become winners for you too.

Angela Nilsen

> The more recipes I lighten up – and the more ways I find to do it – the more I find I prefer my versions to the much richer alternatives

Symbols and charts

To highlight nutritional aspects, there are easily recognizable symbols that determine whether a recipe is low fat, whether it contains one or more of your five a day or by how much sugar has been reduced, for example.

To help you quickly see how I have improved each recipe, nutritional therapist Kerry Torrens has created charts that give you an at-a-glance comparison of calories, fat, sugar or salt per serving in the classic version of the recipe and the lighter one.

LOW FAT
3 g fat or less per 100 g

Guideline Daily Amounts

GDAs are a guide as to how many calories and nutrients we should have as part of a balanced, healthy diet. We all vary in size and activity levels, so these figures are a guide only, but they can help you see how much a food or even a recipe is contributing towards your daily diet.

For adults these are:

FIBRE
One serving supplies one-third of your daily requirements, or at least 6 g fibre per 100 g

Guideline Daily Amounts (GDAs)

	Women	Men
Energy (Kcal)	2000	2500
Protein (g)	45	55
Carbohydrates (g)	230	300
Sugar (g)	90	120
Fat (g)	70	95
Saturates (g)	20	30
Fibre (g)	24	24
Salt (g)	6	6

ONE-THIRD OF THE FAT OF THE CLASSIC RECIPE

LOW IN SATURATED FAT

1.5 g saturates or less per 100 g

LOW SALT

0.3 g salt or less per 100 g

LOW SUGAR

5 g sugar or less per 100 g

LOW CALORIE

500 kcal or less per main course, 150 kcal or less for a starter or dessert

ONE OF YOUR FIVE A DAY

The number of portions of fruit and/or vegetables per serving

FOLIC ACID

One serving supplies at least 30% of your daily requirements

VITAMIN C

One serving supplies at least 30% of your daily requirements

OMEGA 3

One serving supplies at least 30% of your daily requirements

CALCIUM

One serving supplies at least 30% of your daily requirements

IRON

One serving supplies at least 30% of your daily requirements

HALF THE SATURATED FAT OF THE CLASSIC RECIPE

ONE-QUARTER OF THE SALT OF THE CLASSIC RECIPE

HALF THE CALORIES OF THE CLASSIC RECIPE

ONE-FIFTH OF THE SUGAR OF THE CLASSIC RECIPE

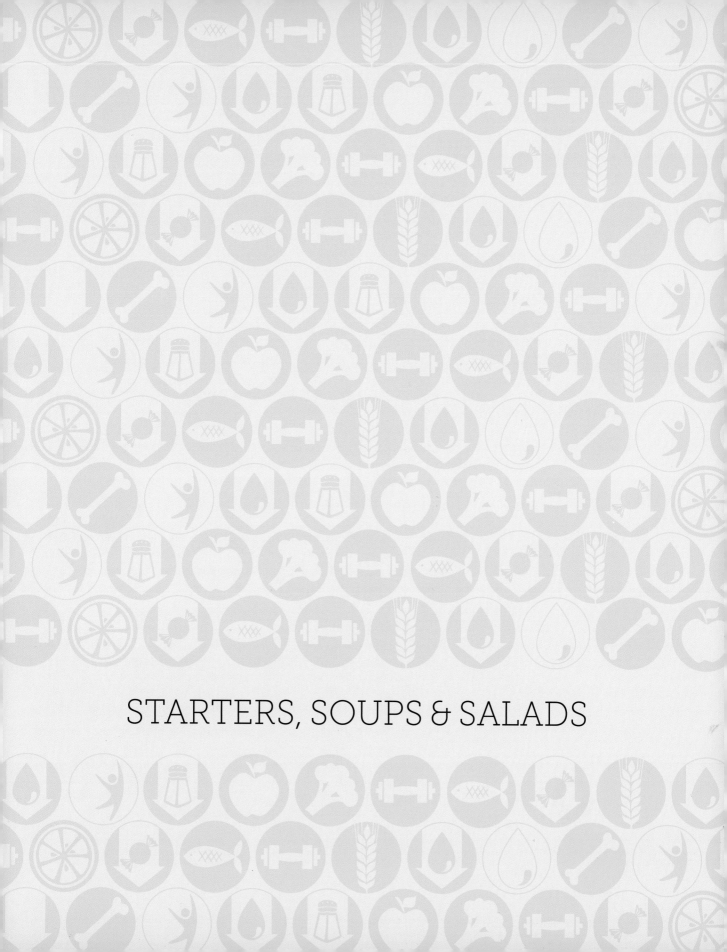

STARTERS, SOUPS & SALADS

Prawn cocktail

This dish is back in fashion, so with a few updated twists, I've given it a lighter, more modern feel. Fromage frais replaces some of the mayonnaise for the classically rich Marie Rose sauce, and mixing in flavours like Tabasco and brandy means less sweet ketchup is needed. In addition, using watercress and avocado instead of iceberg lettuce boosts nutrition.

	Classic	Lighter
Kcals	303	186
Fat	24 g	13 g
Sat fat	4 g	2 g
Salt	1.97 g	1.23 g

Per serving 186 kcals

protein 14 g, carbs 4 g, fat 13 g,
sat fat 2 g, fibre 1 g, sugar 3 g, salt 1.23 g

Serves 4

Prep: 35 minutes

For the salad

650 g (1 lb 7 oz) prawns in their shells, cooked, to give 200 g (7 oz) peeled prawns

2 tablespoons lime juice

100 g (4 oz) cucumber

1 tablespoon white wine vinegar

1 tablespoon snipped dill

1 small ripe avocado

50 g (2 oz) watercress

pinch of cayenne pepper, for sprinkling

For the sauce

2 tablespoons mayonnaise

5 tablespoons fromage frais

1½ tablespoons tomato ketchup

splash of Tabasco sauce

splash of Worcestershire sauce

1 teaspoon brandy

freshly ground black pepper

1 Peel the prawns. Rinse the prawns in a large sieve under a cold tap, then pat dry with kitchen paper. Lay the prawns in a shallow, non-metallic dish and squeeze over 1 tablespoon of the lime juice, then add a twist of pepper. Set aside.

2 Chop the cucumber into small dice and tip into a dish. Spoon over the vinegar, scatter over the dill and a grinding of pepper, then set aside. Halve, stone and peel the avocado, then chop into small dice. Spoon over the rest of the lime juice and toss together gently with a twist of pepper.

3 For the sauce, mix together the mayonnaise, fromage frais and ketchup. Stir in the Tabasco and Worcestershire sauces and brandy with a twist of pepper.

4 To serve, take 4 cocktail glasses and put a small spoonful of the sauce into the bottom of each. Very coarsely chop most of the watercress, leaving a few sprigs whole. Lay the chopped watercress on top of the sauce. Drain the cucumber well and spoon it over the watercress with the avocado. Pile over the prawns, then spoon over the rest of the sauce. Tuck in the whole sprigs of watercress and serve with a sprinkling of cayenne.

substitute some of
the mayonnaise with
fromage frais

French onion soup

You might think this soup doesn't need a makeover, but the rich beef stock, butter (to create the sticky onion caramelization), croutons and Gruyère cheese make this a heavyweight dish. This lighter version is still substantial.

	Classic	Lighter
Kcals	570	405
Fat	32 g	19 g
Sat fat	17 g	5 g
Salt	5.77 g	1 g

Per serving 405 kcals

Protein 12 g, carbs 44 g, fat 19 g, sat fat 5 g, fibre 4 g, sugar 18 g, salt 1 g

Serves 4

Prep: 30 minutes
Cook: 1¼ hours

For the soup

3 tablespoons extra virgin rapeseed oil

4 large Spanish onions, 900 g (2 lb), halved lengthways and thinly sliced

4 sprigs of thyme

2 bay leaves

300 ml (½ pint) dry white wine

1 rounded tablespoon plain flour

1 tablespoon vegetable bouillon powder

For the topping

1 garlic clove, crushed

1 tablespoon extra virgin rapeseed oil

4 diagonal slices baguette

25 g (1 oz) Parmesan cheese, coarsely grated

50 g (2 oz) Gruyère cheese, coarsely grated

salt and freshly ground black pepper

1 Heat a large pan, add the oil and stir in the onions, 3 of the thyme sprigs and the bay leaves, then season with a little salt. Cook over a high heat for 5 minutes, stirring often. The onions shouldn't brown, just start to soften. Lower the heat, then cook slowly for 35 minutes, uncovered, stirring often.

2 Meanwhile, bring the wine to the boil in a small pan, then bubble away for 30 seconds. Leave to cool. Toast the flour in a small heavy pan over a medium heat for a few minutes, stirring occasionally, until light brown. Set aside.

3 When the onions are very soft and reduced, turn up the heat so that they caramelize, then cook for another 12–15 minutes, stirring occasionally. When they are sticky and a rich brown colour, stir in the flour. With the heat still high, gradually pour in the wine and stir. Pour in 1.2 litres (2 pints) cold water, stir in the bouillon powder, then slowly bring to the boil. Skim off any froth. Simmer for 15 minutes so that all the flavours can mingle.

4 While the soup simmers, make the croûtons. Preheat the oven to 200°C (fan 180 °C, 400°F, gas mark 6). Mix the garlic and the oil together. Brush the mixture all over the slices of bread, then cut each one into cubes. Scatter over a baking sheet, then bake for 8–10 minutes until golden. Set aside.

5 Line a baking sheet with baking parchment. Mix the leaves from the remaining thyme sprig with the Parmesan. Spread over the baking sheet into a 13 x 8 cm (5 x 3¼ inch) rectangle. Bake for about 8 minutes until melted and turning golden. Remove, leave to firm up, then snap into jagged pieces.

6 To serve, remove the herbs and ladle the soup into bowls. Scatter over a few croûtons, the Gruyère and some pepper, then perch a Parmesan crisp on top.

use water and a little bouillon powder instead of all beef stock to reduce salt

Twice-baked cheese soufflés

These delicious little make-ahead soufflés miraculously rise again when re-baked. You can prepare them up to 24 hours in advance, making them perfect for entertaining. Switching some of the full-fat ingredients for lower fat ones or for ingredients with stronger flavour helps to transform this into a low-fat recipe.

	Classic	Lighter
Kcals	275	175
Fat	21.6 g	10.6 g
Sat fat	12.5 g	4 g
Salt	0.9 g	0.5 g

Per serving 175 kcals
Protein 9.7 g, carbs 10.4 g, fat 10.6 g, sat fat 4 g, fibre 0.9 g, sugar 4.6 g, salt 0.5 g

Serves 6
Prep: 45 minutes, plus cooling and chilling
Cook: 30 minutes

For the soufflés

1 heaped tablespoon polenta

1½ tablespoons olive oil, plus extra for greasing

1 teaspoon butter

25 g (1 oz) plain flour

250 ml (9 fl oz) semi-skimmed milk

50 g (2 oz) Parmesan cheese, grated

1 teaspoon Dijon mustard

50 g (2 oz) light soft cheese

2 heaped tablespoons snipped chives, plus extra to serve

2 large egg yolks

3 large egg whites

50 g (2 oz) rocket, to serve

For the tomato salsa

350 g (12 oz) cherry tomatoes, finely chopped

½ small red onion, finely chopped

1 teaspoon tomato purée

pinch of crushed dried chillies

freshly ground black pepper

1 Lightly brush 6 x 150 ml (¼ pint) ramekins with olive oil and coat with the polenta, shaking out any excess. Place the ramekins in a small roasting tin. Heat the oil and butter in a medium saucepan, stir in the flour and cook, stirring, for 1 minute. Remove from the heat and pour in the milk, a little at a time, stirring well until the mixture is smooth.

2 Return the pan to the heat and cook, stirring constantly, until the mixture thickens and comes to the boil. Remove from the heat. Reserve 1 heaped tablespoon of the Parmesan and stir the rest into the mixture, with the mustard, then the soft cheese in small spoonfuls. Add the chives, season with pepper and leave to cool slightly.

3 Meanwhile, make the salsa. Mix together the tomatoes, onion, tomato purée and crushed chillies. Season with pepper, cover and chill until ready to serve.

4 Preheat the oven to 200°C (fan 180°C/400°F/gas mark 6). Beat the egg yolks into the cheese mixture. Whisk the egg whites to stiff peaks. Using a large metal spoon, fold a spoonful into the mixture to slacken slightly. Gently and evenly fold in the remaining whites, half at a time, keeping the mixture light and airy. Divide the mixture evenly between the ramekin dishes.

5 Pour enough cold water into the roasting tin to come halfway up the sides of the dishes. Bake for 15–18 minutes until golden on top and risen. Carefully remove from the tin and leave to cool. The soufflés will sink as they cool. Cover the dishes once cold and keep for up to 24 hours in the fridge.

6 To re-cook the soufflés, preheat the oven to 200°C (fan 180°C/400°F/gas mark 6). Remove the soufflés from the fridge about 10 minutes before baking. Turn each out of its dish and place, right-side up, on a baking sheet lined with baking parchment. Sprinkle the reserved Parmesan over each soufflé, then bake for 10 minutes or until risen. Scatter with chives. Serve each with a pile of salsa and rocket.

keep saturated fat down by replacing some of the
butter with olive oil

•

Lower the fat by replacing full-fat milk with
semi-skimmed milk

•

use strong-flavoured Parmesan and a light soft cheese
so you can reduce the fat even more

•

include a tomato salsa to boost your five a day

Salmon pâté

The rich taste and texture of a fish pâté makes it an appealing starter – but this requires a lot of fat. By lightening the load and making a few sneaky ingredient swops, this version becomes heart-friendly, but maintains all the creaminess of the classic. To keep it light when serving, offer torn pieces of toasted or grilled pitta bread.

	Classic	Lighter
Kcals	225	157
Fat	19.2 g	10.1 g
Sat fat	11.8 g	3.5 g
Salt	2.2 g	0.7 g

Per serving 157 kcals

Protein 15.1 g, carbs 1.9 g, fat 10.1 g, sat fat 3.5 g, fibre 0.7 g, sugar 1.6 g, salt 0.7 g

Serves 4

Prep: 15 minutes, plus cooling
Cook: 5 minutes

1 skinless salmon fillet, about 140 g (5 oz)

½ small, ripe avocado, stoned and peeled

175 g (6 oz) light soft cheese

2 teaspoons lemon juice

1 garlic clove, crushed

2 teaspoons snipped chives, plus extra for scattering

salt and freshly ground black pepper

1 Poach the salmon. Lay it in a saucepan, pour over enough water to just cover, then bring to a gentle simmer, cover and poach for about 5 minutes or until just cooked (timing depends on how thick the fish is). Remove from the heat and leave for 2 minutes, still in the water. Lift out the salmon with a slotted spoon and leave until cold.

2 Meanwhile, chop the avocado and place in a food processor with the soft cheese, lemon juice and garlic. Process until smooth.

3 When the salmon is cold, flake it into pieces. Tip the salmon and chives into the food processor with the avocado mix and process again, briefly if you want to keep it slightly chunky, or longer for a smooth pâté. Season with black pepper and a pinch of salt. Spoon into small ramekins or similar dishes and scatter extra chives on top.

Reduce calories and fat by replacing full-fat soft cheese and cream with a mix of avocado and light soft cheese

Prawn laksa

With its fragrantly spiced broth, this South East Asian dish is a tasty starter for 4, or serve it for 2–3 as a light meal. Its richness comes from high-fat coconut milk and its saltiness from fish sauce, stock and prawns. By adjusting ingredients, fat and saturated fat are halved, the salt content is impressively lowered but none of the creaminess is lost.

	Classic	Lighter
Kcals	556	298
Fat	25.4 g	12.6 g
Sat fat	16.0 g	7.4 g
Salt	6.3 g	1.7 g

Per serving 298 kcals

Protein 16.1 g, carbs 29.8 g, fat 12.6 g, sat fat 7.4 g, fibre 4 g, sugar 4.9 g, salt 1.7g

Serves 4 starter bowlfuls

Prep: 20 minutes
Cook: 40 minutes

For the laksa

20 cooked king prawns, in their shells

400 ml (14 fl oz) can reduced-fat coconut milk

2 small pak choi bulbs, sliced into 2.5 cm (1 inch) pieces

100 g (4 oz) mangetout, halved lengthways

100 g (4 oz) thin asparagus spears, trimmed and each diagonally sliced into 4

2 teaspoons rapeseed oil

2 teaspoons fish sauce

½ teaspoon light muscovado sugar

140 g (5 oz) dried medium egg noodles

100 g (4 oz) beansprouts

1 tablespoon lime juice

For the laksa paste

2 plump garlic cloves, roughly grated

1 small shallot, roughly grated

1 lemongrass stalk, tough outer leaves removed, roughly chopped

2.5 cm (1 inch) piece fresh root ginger, roughly grated

1 small Thai red chilli, some seeds removed, or leave in for extra heat

small pinch of turmeric

¼ teaspoon ground cumin

1 tablespoon chopped fresh coriander leaves and their stems

2 teaspoons chilli paste, such as sambal oelek

pinch of salt

To garnish

roughly chopped fresh coriander leaves

1 Make a stock with the prawn shells. Peel the prawns, leaving the tail ends on, and put the shells and heads into a saucepan with 450 ml (16 fl oz) water. Bring to the boil, then lower the heat and simmer gently for 20 minutes. Strain through a sieve to give you about 350 ml (12 fl oz) stock.

2 Meanwhile, make the laksa paste. Put all the ingredients in a mini blender with 2 tablespoons of the coconut milk from the can, then process to as fine a paste as you can. Set aside.

3 Steam the pak choi, mangetout and asparagus together for 3–4 minutes until tender-crisp and still bright green. Set aside. Heat the oil in a wok or large sauté pan, tip in the laksa paste and stir-fry for about 4 minutes. Pour in 300 ml (½ pint) of the prawn stock and simmer for 2 minutes. Stir in the fish sauce, sugar and the rest of the can of coconut milk and simmer gently for 2–3 minutes, being careful not to have the heat too high in case the broth curdles. Remove from the heat.

4 Cook the noodles according to the packet instructions, for about 4–5 minutes. While the noodles are cooking, put the steamed vegetables and the prawns into the broth and return to a low heat to warm them through for 1–2 minutes. Stir in about half of the beansprouts and the rest of the prawn stock if you wish to thin the broth down a bit. Remove from the heat and stir in the lime juice (otherwise it may curdle the broth if overheated).

5 Drain the noodles and twist in piles into 4 small, wide bowls. Ladle the broth over the noodles with the vegetables and prawns, then top with a little pile of the remaining beansprouts and a scattering of coriander.

TIP

- If you want to use raw prawns in their shells instead of cooked, add them to the broth in step 4 just before the vegetables, and simmer for 2–3 minutes until just cooked.

Lower the fat, especially saturated fat, by replacing full-fat coconut milk with light coconut milk

•

Make your own laksa paste and stock so that you can control and reduce the amount of salt

•

Reduce the fish sauce to lower the salt further, and maintain flavour from the variety of ingredients in the laksa paste

Chicken Caesar salad

Salads can fool you. You can get a surprisingly high percentage of calories from the fat in the dressing, croûtons and cheese. In this variation on a classic chicken Caesar salad, fat is kept to a minimum but the dish is still creamy and rich in flavour.

	Classic	Lighter
Kcals	674	430
Fat	47.5 g	23 g
Sat fat	9.2 g	4 g
Salt	2.19 g	1.37 g

Per serving 430 kcals

Protein 43 g, carbs 15 g, fat 23 g, sat fat 4 g, fibre 3 g, sugar 4 g, salt 1.37 g

Serves 4

Prep: 25 minutes, plus marinating
Cook: 25 minutes

For the chicken

1½ tablespoons lemon juice, plus extra for squeezing

1 tablespoon olive oil

2 teaspoons thyme leaves plus a few sprigs

1 garlic clove, bashed to bruise

4 boneless, skinless chicken breasts, about 140 g (5 oz) each

For the croutons

100 g (4 oz) rustic Granary bread

2 tablespoons olive oil

For the dressing and salad

1 garlic clove, finely chopped

1 teaspoon Dijon mustard

½ teaspoon Worcestershire sauce

1 tablespoon lemon juice, plus extra for squeezing

good pinch of crushed dried chillies

4 anchovy fillets in oil, drained and finely chopped

3 tablespoons good-quality mayonnaise

4 tablespoons fat-free natural yogurt

1 head cos lettuce, leaves separated, washed and dried

100 g bag rocket or watercress

25 g (1 oz) piece of Parmesan cheese, shaved (with a potato peeler)

freshly ground black pepper

1 Marinate the chicken. Mix the lemon juice, oil, thyme and garlic in a shallow, non-metallic dish. Add the chicken and turn it over in the marinade to coat well. Season with pepper, cover and leave in the fridge for up to 2 hours.

2 Preheat the oven to 200°C (fan 180°C/400°F/gas mark 6). Slice, then cut the bread into big, rough cubes for the croûtons. Spread them in a single layer on a baking sheet, then brush all over with the oil. Bake for about 10 minutes until golden and crisp.

3 Meanwhile, put the garlic into a mini blender with the mustard, Worcestershire sauce, lemon juice, crushed chillies and anchovies. Blend until smooth, add the mayonnaise and yogurt, then blend again – it should be the consistency of double cream. Adjust the taste with the lemon juice and pepper. If necessary, thin with a couple of teaspoons of cold water to get the consistency right so that it will coat the leaves.

4 Heat a griddle pan until very hot. Lay the chicken on the griddle, on the side that had the skin on. Cook for 15–16 minutes, turning once or twice, until cooked through. Remove, then let the meat sit for 5 minutes before slicing.

5 Keep any small inner lettuce leaves whole, tear the larger outer leaves into 2–3 pieces, then put them all into a large bowl with the rocket or watercress. Pour just under half the dressing over the leaves and carefully toss to coat. Either assemble in the bowl, or pile the leaves on to individual plates, tucking in the croûtons, chicken and Parmesan. Drizzle the rest of the dressing over and around, then finish with an extra squeeze of lemon.

A mixture of mayonnaise and fat-free yogurt make a delicious low-fat dressing

•

Bake rather than fry croûtons; griddle rather than fry chicken

•

Use good-quality anchovies and Parmesan for flavour, so that no salt is needed for seasoning

•

Add rocket to the cos lettuce to boost vitamin C and the B vitamin folate

Creamy butternut squash soup

By changing to a healthier cooking technique and considering different ways to add flavour, the comfort factor for this soup remains intact – yet fat and salt are greatly lowered.

	Classic	Lighter
Kcals	436	213
Fat	29.7 g	6.2 g
Sat fat	13.1 g	0.9 g
Salt	1.2 g	0.1 g

Per serving 213 kcals

Protein 6.6 g, carbs 34.1 g, fat 6.2 g, sat fat 0.9 g, fibre 8.8 g, sugar 20.1 g, salt 0.1 g

Serves 4

Prep: 30 minutes
Cook: 45 minutes

1½ teaspoons coriander seeds

1 teaspoon cumin seeds

1 butternut squash, about 1.25 kg (2 lb 12 oz)

1 large onion, peeled

1 red pepper, cored, deseeded and cut into 3–4 cm (1¼–1½ inch) chunks

3 garlic cloves, peeled and halved

¼ teaspoon dried crushed chillies

1 tablespoon rapeseed oil plus 2 teaspoons

850 ml (1½ pints) hot vegetable bouillon or stock

4 tablespoons natural yogurt

freshly ground black pepper

1 Preheat the oven to 200°C (fan 180°C/400°F/gas mark 6). Heat a small dry, heavy pan, tip in the coriander and cumin seeds and toast for a couple of minutes in the pan until they start to smell fragrant (they will also start to pop in the pan), shaking the pan often so that they don't burn. Grind the seeds to a fine powder using a pestle and mortar. Set aside.

2 Halve the squash widthways and remove the peel with a vegetable peeler. Slice each piece of squash in half lengthways, scoop out and discard the seeds, then slice it into 3–4 cm (1¼–1½ inch) chunks. Put the squash in a large roasting tin. Halve the onion lengthways, then cut each half into about 8 thin wedges. Scatter into the tin with the red pepper and garlic.

3 Mix the ground spices and crushed chillies with all of the oil, pour it over the vegetables and toss together so that they are all well coated (hands are good for this). Spread them out into a single layer, as they will roast better than if they are overcrowded. Season with a good grating of black pepper. Roast for 40–45 minutes or until the vegetables are very tender and tinged brown on the edges.

4 Remove from the oven, then pour 300 ml (½ pint) boiling water into the roasting tin, stirring to scrape up any sticky bits from the bottom of the tin. Stir in 500 ml (18 fl oz) of the stock. Carefully transfer (in batches if necessary) to a blender or food processor and purée until smooth.

5 Pour into a saucepan and stir in the remaining stock. Reheat. To serve, drop a spoonful of the yogurt on top of each bowlful and swirl it through the soup to make it creamy.

Reduce saturated fat with simple swaps – rapeseed oil replaces butter for cooking, yogurt replaces cream for added creaminess

Salad Niçoise

With salty ingredients such as anchovies and a generous amount of dressing, salt, fat and calories can soon creep up in a salad Niçoise. But there are ways to make healthier changes and retain its character.

	Classic	Lighter
Kcals	621	451
Fat	43 g	28.3 g
Sat fat	7.6 g	4.9 g
Salt	2.7 g	1.7 g

Per serving 451 kcals

Protein 39 g, carbs 8.8 g, fat 28.3 g, sat fat 4.9 g, fibre 9 g, sugar 4.8 g, salt 1.7 g

Serves 4

Prep: 30 minutes
Cook: 15–20 minutes

For the salad

300 g (11 oz) green beans, trimmed

200 g (8 oz) podded broad beans, fresh or frozen

4 medium eggs

4 x 115 g (4 oz) tuna steaks, cut 2.5 cm (1 inch) thick

1 teaspoon rapeseed oil

250 g (9 oz) cherry tomatoes, halved

12 pieces of chargrilled artichokes in oil, well drained

16 small black olives

4 anchovy fillets in oil, drained and finely chopped

For the dressing

1 small garlic clove

1 tablespoon lemon juice

1 tablespoon white wine vinegar

1 teaspoon Dijon mustard

2 tablespoons extra virgin olive oil

2 tablespoons rapeseed oil

1 tablespoon flat leaf parsley

2 tablespoons snipped chives

salt and freshly ground black pepper

1 Cook the green beans in boiling water for 3–5 minutes or until tender-crisp and bright green. Drain into a sieve and cool quickly under running cold water. Cook the broad beans in boiling water for about 3 minutes, then drain and cool as before. Pop the broad beans out of their skins. Set aside.

2 Put the eggs in a medium saucepan, cover well with water and bring to a boil, then time them for 5 minutes (for soft-boiled). Immediately drain and cool in cold water to stop them cooking further. Leave for few minutes, then peel off the shells. Set aside.

3 To make the dressing, crush the garlic into a small bowl, then whisk in the lemon juice, vinegar and mustard. Gradually whisk in the olive oil, then the rapeseed oil. Stir in the herbs and season with pepper and a pinch of salt.

4 Pat the tuna steaks dry with kitchen paper, then rub them all over with the rapeseed oil. Season with pepper. Heat a griddle pan or non-stick frying pan, then lay the tuna steaks in the pan and cook for 2–3 minutes on each side (for medium-rare). Remove and set aside.

5 To assemble each salad, scatter a quarter of the green beans, broad beans, tomatoes, artichokes, olives and anchovies in each of 4 wide, shallow bowls. Lay a tuna steak on top along with 2 egg halves, then drizzle over the dressing.

choose fresh tuna steak over canned to retain more of its 'good' fat and griddle rather than fry it so that less oil is needed

Leek and potato soup

Loved for its richness and silky smooth texture, the reliance on double cream to provide that for this classic soup can make it very high in fat. Using a creative choice of ingredients, this version offers a much healthier alternative that has all the creaminess and flavour but far fewer calories and less fat.

	Classic	Lighter
Kcals	428	141
Fat	32.3 g	4.9 g
Sat fat	20 g	1.1 g
Salt	1.3 g	0.2 g

Per serving 141 kcals

Protein 5.4 g, carbs 18.5 g, fat 4.9 g, sat fat 1.1g, fibre 4.9g, sugar 5.1g, salt 0.2g

Serves 4

Prep: 15 minutes
Cook: 15 minutes

1 tablespoons rapeseed oil

1 small onion, chopped

2–3 leeks, trimmed, cleaned and sliced (300 g/10 oz total prepared weight)

300 g (11 oz) potato, such as King Edward, cut into 2 cm (¾ inch) cubes

140 g (5 oz) cauliflower, cut into 2 cm (¾ inch) pieces

1 litre (1¾ pints) vegetable stock from a good-quality bouillon powder

50 ml (2fl oz) semi-skimmed milk

4 teaspoons half-fat crème fraîche

snipped chives, to garnish

freshly ground black pepper

1 Heat the oil in a large saucepan. Tip in the onion and leeks and fry for 4–5 minutes or until both are beginning to soften. Stir in the potato and cauliflower, season with pepper, then pour in the stock. Bring to a simmer and cook for 8–10 minutes or until all the vegetables are very tender. They should be very soft, but not overcooked or they will lose their freshness.

2 Transfer the mixture to a food processor or blender and purée until smooth. Do this in batches if necessary. Stir in the milk. Pour into a clean pan to briefly reheat, or if you prefer a really smooth texture, pour and press the soup through a fine sieve first.

3 Pour into bowls, spoon and swirl in 1 teaspoon crème fraîche through each and serve scattered with chives and an extra grating of pepper.

TIP

• To clean the leeks, slit each one lengthways just deep enough so that you can open it out, then rinse them under cold running water to wash out any grit or soil.

Instead of cream, use cauliflower, milk and half-fat crème fraîche to provide the creaminess and drop the calories, fat and saturated fat right down

Potato salad

It's not the potatoes that make this picnic classic unhealthy; the problem is all the mayonnaise and cream. This homemade version is easy and just as satisfying. Keep the potato skins on to boost the fibre.

	Classic	Lighter
Kcals	370	215
Fat	32.4 g	12.1 g
Sat fat	3.7 g	2.7 g
Salt	0.9 g	0.5 g

Per serving 215 kcals

Protein 4.5 g, carbs 21.9 g, fat 12.1 g, sat fat 2.7 g, fibre 2 g, sugar 4.5 g, salt 0.5 g

Serves 6

Prep: 10 minutes
Cook: 10 minutes

750 g (1 lb 10 oz) Charlotte new potatoes, unpeeled and scrubbed

2 tablespoons good-quality mayonnaise

3 tablespoons natural yogurt

3 tablespoons half-fat crème fraîche

1 teaspoon Dijon mustard

1 tablespoon semi-skimmed milk

8 spring onions, ends trimmed, halved lengthways and sliced

3 tablespoons snipped chives

1 tablespoon chopped tarragon

salt and freshly ground black pepper

1 Cut the potatoes into 2.5–3 cm (1–1¼ inch) chunks so that they are all the same size and will cook evenly. Put them in a pan of boiling water. Once the water has returned to the boil, lower the heat slightly and cook for about 10 minutes or until just cooked and still keeping their shape. Tip them into a colander to drain well, then transfer to a large serving bowl.

2 While the potatoes are cooking, mix together the mayonnaise, yogurt, crème fraîche, mustard and milk. Add the spring onions, then most of the chives and tarragon to the potatoes. Season with pepper and a pinch of salt.

3 Spoon the dressing over the potatoes while they are still warm, then toss gently together so that they are well coated but don't break up. Scatter over the remaining chives and tarragon. Cover and chill in the fridge. For the best flavour, remove from the fridge 15–20 minutes before serving.

use mayo with yogurt and half-fat crème fraîche for a creamy-tasting, but low-fat dressing

Coronation chicken

Originally created for a celebratory lunch for the coronation of HM Queen Elizabeth II in 1953, this British dish is a curious mix of East meets West. For a contemporaray take on a classic, I've come up with this lighter version using fresh, modern ingredients. As an alternative to rice try serving it with couscous mixed with chopped fresh coriander leaves instead.

	Classic	Lighter
Kcals	797	402
Fat	65 g	23 g
Sat fat	14 g	5 g
Salt	1.53 g	0.53 g

Per serving 402 kcals

Protein 35.2 g, carbs 15 g, fat 23 g, sat fat 5 g, fibre 3 g, sugar 14 g, salt 0.53 g

Serves 6

Prep: 30 minutes, plus cooling
Cook: 2 hours 5 minutes

For the chicken

1.6 kg (3 lb 8 oz) whole chicken

2 small onions, roughly chopped

1 carrot, roughly sliced

4 sprigs of tarragon

2 bay leaves

For the sauce

1 tablespoon rapeseed oil

4 teaspoons medium curry powder

2 teaspoons tomato purée

6 soft dried apricots, quartered

1 teaspoon light muscovado sugar

1 tablespoon lime juice

100 g (4 oz) mayonnaise

250 g (9 oz) fromage frais, virtually fat free

For the salad

6 spring onions

25 g (1 oz) fresh coriander, leaves only, chopped

1 ripe medium mango, stoned, peeled and sliced

100 g (4 oz) watercress

freshly ground black pepper

1 Put the chicken in a large pan, then pour in enough cold water to just cover. Drop half the chopped onion into the pan with the carrot, tarragon and bay leaves. Cover and bring to the boil, then lower to a gentle simmer for about 1¾ hours or until the chicken is cooked (the legs will fall easily away from the body). Remove from the heat, but leave the chicken in the liquid to cool for about 3 hours. When cold, lift the chicken out of the stock, then strain (skim off any fat from the stock) and keep 200 ml (7 fl oz) for the sauce. This can be done a day ahead and chilled. The excess stock can be chilled, then frozen.

2 To make the sauce, heat the oil in a small saucepan, tip in the remaining chopped onion and fry for about 5–8 minutes until softened and pale golden. Stir in the curry powder and cook for 1 minute, stirring. Pour in the reserved chicken stock, then stir in the tomato purée. Cover and simmer for 10 minutes.

3 Meanwhile, put the apricots in a small pan with enough water to just cover them, then simmer for 15 minutes. Drain, reserving 1 tablespoon of the liquid. Purée the apricots in a small blender with the reserved liquid, then press through a sieve (you should get about 1 tablespoon purée).

4 Remove the curry sauce from the heat, then stir in the sugar. Strain through a sieve, pressing as much through as you can with a wooden spoon, then stir in the lime juice and apricot purée and leave until cold.

5 Mix together the mayonnaise and fromage frais, then stir in the cold curry sauce. Season to taste with a good grinding of pepper.

6 Cut the spring onions into long, slim slivers, then set aside. If you want them to curl, put into a bowl of iced water while you finish the salad. Remove the skin from the chicken. Strip the meat off the bones in chunky pieces, remove the breasts separately and thickly slice. Gently toss the chicken with the curried sauce, the coriander and most of the mango. Scatter the watercress on to a platter. Spoon the chicken mix on top, tuck in the rest of the mango and finish with a pile of (drained) spring onion slivers.

Lower fat by replacing some mayo with fromage frais

•

Poach the chicken and remove the skin
to reduce fat further

•

Add flavour with coriander, mango and watercress

Greek salad

This fresh-tasting, crunchy salad is not short on healthy ingredients, but you do need to watch the level of salt from the olives and feta cheese, and fat from the amount of oil used in the dressing. With a few tweaks, twists and additions designed to keep the salad interestingly flavoured, fat, salt and calories have all been lowered.

	Classic	Lighter
Kcals	350	254
Fat	30.9 g	18.6 g
Sat fat	9.8 g	6.3 g
Salt	2.2 g	1.7 g

Per serving 254 kcals

Protein 8.7 g, carbs 12.8 g, fat 18.6 g, sat fat 6.3 g, fibre 5.6 g, sugar 11.1 g, salt 1.7g

Serves 4

Prep: 20 minutes, plus cooling
 and marinating
Cook: 35 minutes

2 red peppers

2 tablespoons extra virgin olive oil

1 tablespoon rapeseed oil

1½ tablespoons lemon juice

½ teaspoon dried oregano

½ cucumber

450 g (1 lb) vine-ripened tomatoes

½ small red onion, peeled

85 g (3 oz) watercress

12 kalamata olives

140 g (5 oz) Greek feta cheese

2 small sprigs of fresh oregano and mint, leaves stripped and roughly chopped

salt and freshly ground black pepper

1 Preheat the oven to 200°C (fan 180°C/400°F/gas mark 6). Put a piece of baking parchment on to a small baking sheet, lay the whole peppers on it and roast them for about 35 minutes, turning occasionally, or until softened and the skins are blackened all over.

2 Transfer the peppers to a heatproof bowl, cover tightly with clingfilm and leave to cool. The steam that is created in the bowl will make the peppers easier to peel. When the peppers are cool enough to handle, remove them from the bowl and peel off the skins, keeping any juices in the bowl. Pull the peppers open, pour any more inside juices into the bowl and remove and discard the cores and seeds. Cut the peppers into strips and lay them in a shallow non-metallic dish.

3 Make the dressing. Pour both the oils and the lemon juice into the bowl with the pepper juices. Whisk them together with the dried oregano and season with pepper and a pinch of salt. Pour this dressing over the peppers, cover and leave to marinate for at least 15 minutes or overnight if you prefer.

4 To serve, chop the cucumber and tomatoes into chunky pieces. Halve the onion half lengthways, then, with the cut face down on the chopping board, slice into wafer-thin slices. Roughly chop the watercress and divide it between 4 bowls. Scatter the cucumber, tomato chunks, onion slices and olives over the top. Crumble the feta into bite-sized pieces and scatter it over each salad. Spoon the marinaded peppers over and finish with a grinding of pepper and the fresh oregano and mint, then let the salad sit for a few minutes for the flavours to blend before serving.

include peppers to increase the vitamin c and flavour, and watercress to improve folate and up your five a day

Fish chowder

A great recipe for a simple, light supper. The real bonus here is that the creamy broth contains significantly less saturated fat than can be found in a classic equivalent using double cream. Adding the fresh thyme, crushed chillies and prosciutto gives the dish an extra kick and reduces the need for too much salt.

	Classic	Lighter
Kcals	482	398
Fat	25.2 g	15.4 g
Sat fat	11.2 g	3.3 g
Salt	2.2 g	0.9 g

Per serving 398 kcals

Protein 31.9 g, carbs 32.1 g, fat 15.4 g, sat fat 3.3 g, fibre 7.1 g, sugar 4.5 g, salt 0.9 g

Serves 4

Prep: 20 minutes
Cook: 35 minutes

1½ tablespoons rapeseed oil

3 slices prosciutto, trimmed of excess fat, cut into strips

2–3 leeks (300 g/11 oz total weight), trimmed, cleaned and thinly sliced

2 plump garlic cloves, finely chopped

3 sprigs of thyme (preferably lemon thyme), plus extra leaves to garnish

2 bay leaves

650 g (1 lb 7 oz) floury potatoes such as Desirée, unpeeled, scrubbed and sliced 5 mm (¼ inch) thick

600 ml (1 pint) hot vegetable stock from a good-quality cube or bouillon powder

good pinch of crushed dried chillies

250 g (9 oz) skinless salmon fillets

250 g (9 oz) skinless pollack or haddock fillets

3 tablespoons half-fat crème fraîche

salt and freshly ground black pepper

snipped chives, to garnish

1   Heat 1 tablespoon of the oil in a large, deep sauté pan. Tip in the prosciutto and fry for 2 minutes until crisp. Remove with a slotted spoon, letting any excess oil drain back into the pan. Set aside. Add the rest of the oil to the pan and fry the leeks, garlic, thyme and bay leaves for 2–3 minutes until the leeks start to soften but still have their vivid colour.

2   Add the potatoes and fry for 2 minutes, turning occasionally. Pour in the stock, plus an extra 100 ml (3½ fl oz) boiling water, and gently press the potatoes down so that they are just covered. Bring to the boil. Boil quite vigorously, uncovered, over a high heat for 10 minutes until the potatoes are almost cooked. The liquid should have thickened very slightly. Scatter in the crushed chillies, some pepper and a pinch of salt.

3   Lower the heat to medium and lay the fish fillets on top of the potatoes. Season the fish with pepper and gently press down so that the fillets are only just submerged. Cover and simmer for about 5 minutes or until the fish is almost cooked. Remove from the heat and allow to sit for another 5–10 minutes. Remove the thyme and bay leaves. Still off the heat, spoon in the crème fraîche and gently swirl around until the broth looks creamy.

4   To serve, gently reheat. Divide the potatoes and fish in large pieces into shallow bowls. Spoon the broth around and scatter with chives, thyme leaves and the prosciutto.

use salmon as well as white fish to give this dish a good helping of omega-3 fatty acids, which are good for heart health

HEALTHY, SATISFYING FAMILY MEALS

Risotto with squash and sage

A bowl of classic Italian risotto can be a healthy option – if you cut back on the fat, you can still achieve the rich creaminess we all associate with this comfort-food favourite.

	Classic	Lighter
Kcals	725	517
Fat	32 g	15 g
Sat fat	16 g	5 g
Salt	3.37 g	0.37 g

Per serving 517 kcals

Protein 15 g, carbs 85 g, fat 15 g, sat fat 5 g, fibre 5 g, sugar 10 g, salt 0.37 g

Serves 4

Prep: 35 minutes
Cook: 35–40 minutes

2 litres (3½ pints) low-salt vegetable stock

4 slices dried porcini mushroom

2½ tablespoons olive oil

1 onion, finely chopped

2 garlic cloves, finely chopped

6 sage leaves, finely chopped, plus extra leaves to garnish

2 sprigs of thyme

½ butternut squash, about 700 g (1 lb 9 oz), peeled, deseeded and cut into 2.5 cm (1 inch) cubes

350 g (12 oz) carnaroli or arborio rice

100 ml (3½ fl oz) dry white wine

handful of flat leaf parsley, chopped

50 g (2 oz) Parmesan cheese, grated

2 tablespoons light mascarpone cheese

freshly ground black pepper

1 Pour the stock into a pan, add the porcini, then bring to a gentle simmer.

2 Heat 2 tablespoons of the oil in a heavy, wide pan. Add the onion, garlic, sage, thyme and squash, then gently fry for about 10 minutes until the squash is almost tender, stirring occasionally, so that it doesn't stick or burn. With the heat on medium, tip the rice into the pan. Keep stirring for 3–4 minutes to toast it without colouring. Pour in the wine and stir everything for 1 minute.

3 Start to add the hot stock (leaving the porcini behind) – this should take 18–20 minutes. Stir in 1½ ladlefuls and adjust the heat so that it simmers. Keep stirring and scraping down the sides of the pan. Once the first ladleful of stock has been absorbed, add another, continuing to stir to keep the risotto creamy. Continue adding and stirring in a ladleful of stock as each previous one is absorbed (it's ready for more when you drag the spoon across the bottom of the pan and it leaves a clear line). As the last of the stock goes in (keep a little back), check if the rice is ready – it should be soft with a slight bite – and the consistency fluid. Season with pepper.

4 Take the pan off the heat. Add the final splash of stock to keep the risotto moist, scatter over the parsley and half of the Parmesan, then spoon on the mascarpone. With the lid on, let the risotto sit for 3–4 minutes to rest.

5 Meanwhile, heat the remaining oil in a small frying pan. Add the extra sage leaves, then fry for a few seconds until starting to colour. Transfer to kitchen paper with a slotted spoon to drain. Spoon the risotto into bowls, then scatter over the rest of the Parmesan and the crisp sage leaves.

Try a small amount of light mascarpone for richness instead of extra Parmesan

Moussaka

With its layers of meaty sauce, fried aubergine and cheesy béchamel, there is a lot to lighten in this dish. However, you can still keep the aubergine rich without frying and using lots of fat. With a few other changes to make the layers still complement each other but in a lighter way, the topping remains tangy, the meat light and spicy and the aubergine creamy.

	Classic	Lighter
Kcals	820	325
Fat	58 g	15 g
Sat fat	24 g	5 g
Salt	1.06 g	0.65 g

Per serving 325 kcals

Protein 28 g, carbs 19 g, fat 15 g, sat fat 5 g, fibre 6 g, sugar 14 g, salt 0.65 g

Serves 6

Prep: 30 minutes
Cook: 2 hours 5 minutes

2½ tablespoons olive oil

1 onion, chopped

2 plump garlic cloves, finely chopped

2 large carrots (about 350 g/12 oz total weight), diced

450 g (1 lb) 5% fat beef mince

100 ml (3½ fl oz) dry white wine

1 teaspoon ground cinnamon, plus extra for sprinkling

¼ teaspoon ground allspice

400 g (14 oz) can plum tomatoes

2 tablespoons tomato purée

1 heaped tablespoon chopped oregano leaves

2 good handfuls of chopped flat leaf parsley, plus extra to garnish

1 tablespoon lemon juice

3 aubergines (about 750 g/1 lb 10 oz total weight), trimmed

For the topping

2 medium eggs

300 g (11 oz) 2% fat Greek yogurt

1 tablespoon cornflour

50 g (2 oz) Parmesan cheese, grated

halved cherry tomatoes, thinly sliced red onion and rocket salad, to serve

salt and freshly ground black pepper

1 Heat 1 tablespoon of the oil in a large, wide sauté pan. Tip in the onion and garlic, then fry for 6–8 minutes until turning golden. Add the carrots and fry for 2 minutes more. Stir the meat into the pan, breaking it up as you stir. Cook and stir over a high heat until the meat is no longer pink.

2 Pour in the wine and briefly cook until most of the liquid has evaporated. Stir in the cinnamon and allspice. Tip in the tomatoes, tomato purée and 1 tablespoon water (mixed with any juices left in the can), then stir to break up the tomatoes. Season with some pepper, add the oregano and half of the parsley and cover, then simmer on a low heat for 50 minutes, stirring occasionally. Season to taste. Mix in the remaining parsley. The sauce can be refrigerated overnight at this stage.

3 While the meat cooks (unless you are doing this a day ahead), prepare the aubergines. Preheat the oven to 200°C (fan 180°C/400°F/gas mark 6). Brush a little of the remaining oil on to 2 large baking sheets. Mix the rest of the oil with the lemon juice. Slice the aubergines into 1 cm (½ inch) thick lengthways slices, then lay them on the oiled baking sheets. Brush with the oil and lemon mix, then season with pepper. Bake for 20–25 minutes until soft, then set aside. Reduce the oven temperature to 180°C (fan 160°C/350°F/gas mark 4).

4 Spread 2 big spoonfuls of the meat mixture on the bottom of an ovenproof dish (about 28 x 20 x 6 cm/11 x 8 x 2½ inches). Lay the aubergine slices on top, slightly overlapping. Spoon the rest of the meat mixture on top.

5 Beat the eggs in a bowl. Spoon a little of the yogurt into a separate bowl and stir in the cornflour, then stir in the remaining yogurt. Mix this into the eggs with half of the cheese. Season with pepper. Pour and spread this over the meat to cover it. Sprinkle with the rest of the cheese, a little cinnamon and a grinding of pepper. Bake for 50 minutes–1 hour until bubbling and golden.

6 Leave the moussaka to stand for 8–10 minutes, then scatter over some chopped parsley and cut into squares. Serve with a salad of tomato, red onion and rocket.

use five per cent fat beef mince to lower fat

•

Bulk out mince with carrot

•

Reduce oil for frying aubergines by baking instead

•

Try a yogurt-based sauce instead of béchamel cheese sauce

•

up the meat sauce flavour with extra spices, fresh herbs and wine to reduce salt

Fish and chips with crushed mushy peas

I was determined to make this popular fast-food dish healthier without compromising on taste and texture – especially since whenever I asked people why they liked it so much, the crisp, deep-fried batter always got a glowing mention. For this fresher version, both fish and chips are light and crisp without being at all greasy.

	Classic	Lighter
Kcals	915	649
Fat	36 g	27 g
Sat fat	11.5 g	4 g
Salt	2.1 g	0.87 g

Per serving 649 kcals

Protein 41 g, carbohydrate 64 g, fat 27g, saturated fat 4 g, fibre 7 g, sugar 4 g, salt 0.87 g

Serves 4

Prep: about 25 minutes
Cook: 40 minutes

For the chips

800 g (1 lb 12 oz) even-sized King Edward or Maris Piper potatoes, unpeeled

2 tablespoons olive oil

For the peas

300 g (11 oz) frozen peas

1 tablespoon olive oil

2 teaspoons lemon juice

For the fish

4 even-sized pieces skinless haddock, hake or cod fillet, about 650 g (1 lb 7oz) total weight

50 g (2 oz) self-raising flour, plus 1 tablespoon

50 g (2 oz) cornflour

1 medium egg white

125 ml (4 fl oz) ice-cold sparkling water

600 ml (1 pint) sunflower oil, for frying

1 lemon, cut into wedges

salt and freshly ground black pepper

1 Scrub the potatoes, cut them lengthways into 1.5 cm (½ inch) thick slices, then cut each slice into 1.5 cm (½ inch) thick chips. Tip the chips into a large saucepan, pour in enough water to just cover and bring to the boil, then lower the heat and gently simmer for 4 minutes. Drain, tip on to a clean tea towel and pat dry, then leave to cool. This can be done 1–2 hours ahead.

2 Preheat the oven to 220°C (fan 200°C/425°F/gas mark 7). Put 1 tablespoon of the olive oil in a large, shallow non-stick roasting tray and heat in the oven for 10 minutes.

3 Transfer the chips to a bowl and toss in the remaining oil using your hands. Tip out in a single layer into the hot roasting tray. Roast for 10 minutes, then turn them over. Roast for 5 more minutes, then turn again. Roast for a final 5–8 minutes until crisp. Drain on kitchen paper.

4 While the chips are in the oven, cook the peas in boiling water for 4 minutes, then drain, tip into the pan and lightly crush with the back of a fork. Mix in the oil, lemon juice and freshly ground pepper. Cover and set aside.

5 The fish can also be cooked while the chips are in the oven. Pat the fillets dry with kitchen paper. Put the 1 tablespoon flour on a plate and use to coat each fillet, patting off the excess. Mix together the remaining flour, cornflour, a pinch of salt and some pepper. Lightly whisk the egg white with a balloon whisk until frothy and bubbly, but not too stiff. Pour the water into the flour mix, gently and briefly whisking as you go. The batter shouldn't be completely smooth. Add the egg white, then lightly whisk in just to mix. Try and keep as many bubbles as you can so that the batter stays light.

6 Pour the oil for frying into a heavy, medium non-stick wok or wok-shaped pan. Preheat to 200°C (400°F) (use a thermometer so that you can check the oil stays at that temperature). Cook 2 pieces of fish at a time, dip them in the batter to coat and let some of it drip off, then lower into the hot oil using a slotted spoon. Fry for 5–6 minutes, making sure the oil stays at 200°C (400°F) and turning the fish over halfway through so that it is golden all over. Lift out with a slotted spoon, drain on kitchen paper and keep hot. Check the oil temperature is 200°C (400°F), then repeat with the remaining fish. Reheat the peas and serve with the fish, chips and lemon wedges.

keep the skin on potatoes to increase the fibre content

•

cut fat chips and oven roast them to reduce fat

•

use a non-stick wok for frying the fish,
and thoroughly drain the cooked fish and chips

•

make a fat-free, tempura-style batter

•

serve with peas and lemon to boost vitamin c

Fish cakes

Creating a golden crispy coating for a fish cake is hard to achieve without using lots of butter or oil to fry it in. By changing the cooking method and using the oven instead of the frying pan, this recipe has been transformed into a healthy low-fat supper with lots of crunch appeal.

	Classic	Lighter
Kcals	370	239
Fat	17.9 g	5 g
Sat fat	4.6 g	0.6 g
Salt	1.9 g	0.7 g

Per serving 239 kcals

Protein 25.8g, carbs 22.6g, fat 5.0g, sat fat 0.6g, fibre 1.9g, sugar 0.9g, salt 0.7g

Makes 4

Prep: 35 minutes, plus cooling and chilling
Cook: 30 minutes

450 g (1 lb) skinless haddock fillet

1 tablespoon rapeseed oil, plus extra for greasing

300 g (10 oz) floury potatoes, such as Maris Piper or King Edward, chopped into 4 cm (1½ inch) chunks

1 tablespoon chopped parsley

2 tablespoons snipped chives

½ teaspoon finely grated lemon zest

1 teaspoon drained capers, finely chopped

½ teaspoon Dijon mustard

1 medium egg

50 g (2 oz) white breadcrumbs

1½ teaspoons plain flour, for shaping

salt and freshly ground black pepper

lemon wedges to serve

1 Preheat the oven to 200°C (fan 180°C/400°F/gas mark 6). Lightly brush the centre of a large piece of foil with a little rapeseed oil. Lay the fish on the oiled foil, season with pepper, then wrap it up and seal to make a parcel. Place on a baking sheet and bake for 12–15 minutes or until just cooked. Unwrap the parcel and set aside to cool.

2 While the fish is baking, cook the potatoes in boiling water for 10–12 minutes or until tender. Drain, return to the dry pan and let them dry out for 1 minute on a very low heat, then remove and mash with a fork. Mix in the parsley, chives, lemon zest, capers and mustard, then season with pepper and a pinch of salt.

3 Drain the fish from its parcel then, flake it into big chunks. Gently stir the fish into the potato without breaking it up. Set aside to cool.

4 Beat the egg on a large plate and spread the breadcrumbs on another plate. Divide the fish cake mixture into 4. On a lightly floured surface or board, shape the mixture into 4 rounds, about 2.5 cm (1 inch) thick. Dip each cake in the egg to coat, then cover all over with the breadcrumbs. Pat to reshape and chill for 20 minutes, or overnight.

5 Heat the oven to 190°C (fan 170°C/375°F/gas mark 5). For each fish cake, spoon ½ teaspoon of the oil in a circle on a non-stick baking tray (with sides to contain the oil when cooking). Sit each fish cake on a circle of oil and drizzle ¼ teaspoon oil over the top of each one. Bake for 10 minutes, then turn each one over once golden and bake for a further 5–8 minutes until also golden underneath.

oven bake rather than fry the fish cakes to lower the fat, and use a non-stick baking tray so that minimum oil is needed

Quiche Lorraine

Butter, cream, lardons, eggs and yolks are all high in fat and the crisp, flaky pastry is key to this recipe. However, there are ways of balancing the right kinds of fats to achieve a great-tasting lighter quiche.

	Classic	Lighter
Kcals	525	272
Fat	45 g	17 g
Sat fat	25 g	6 g
Salt	1.21 g	0.92 g

Per serving 272 kcals

Protein 13 g, carbs 19 g, fat 17 g, sat fat 6 g, fibre 1 g, sugar 2 g, salt 0.92 g

Serves 8

Prep: 35 minutes plus chilling
Cook: 45–55 minutes

For the pastry

175 g (6 oz) plain flour, plus extra for dusting

6 tablespoons Greek yogurt

4 tablespoons extra virgin olive oil

1 garlic clove, finely crushed

For the filling

175 g (6 oz) lean, freshly sliced good-quality ham, trimmed of all fat (cut about 1 cm/½ inch thick)

50 g (2 oz) Gruyère cheese

3 large eggs

200 ml (7 fl oz) half-fat crème fraîche

125 ml (4 fl oz) full-fat milk

good pinch of ground or freshly grated nutmeg, plus extra for sprinkling

salt and freshly ground black pepper

1 For the pastry, put the flour in a bowl with the yogurt, olive oil, garlic, a pinch of salt and a generous grinding of pepper. Using a table knife, mix to a dough, then briefly knead until smooth.

2 Roll the pastry out on a lightly floured surface, as thinly as you can, then use it to line a 23 cm (9 inch) round, 2.5 cm (1 inch) deep, loose-bottomed fluted flan tin. Trim the pastry edges with scissors so that the pastry sits slightly above the tin, then wrap and reserve the trimmings. Press the pastry into the flutes of the tin. Lightly prick the base with a fork and chill for 10 minutes. Preheat the oven to 200°C (fan 180°C/400°F/gas mark 6) and put in a baking sheet to heat.

3 Line the pastry base with foil, shiny side down, fill with dried beans, then bake on the hot baking sheet for 15 minutes. Remove the foil and beans, then bake for 5–7 minutes more or until the pastry is slightly golden all over and no longer raw on the base. Remove from the oven and, if any small cracks have appeared in the pastry, patch them up with the reserved pastry trimmings.

4 Meanwhile, prepare the filling. Cut the ham into cubes. Cut half of the cheese into cubes and finely grate the rest. Beat the eggs with a fork, then beat in the crème fraîche, followed by the milk. Season with nutmeg and pepper.

5 Scatter the ham and cheese over the cooked pastry base. Pour the egg mixture over, then sprinkle with a little more nutmeg. Put the tart into the oven, then lower the heat to 190°C (fan 170°C/375°F/gas mark 5). Bake for 25–30 minutes or until softly set and tinged golden. Leave to settle for 5 minutes before removing from the tin. Serve while warm and softly set – it's also good cold.

use olive oil and Greek yogurt instead of butter and egg yolks to make pastry

Chicken korma

My challenge with this recipe was to create creaminess without cream, but also to delve into its heritage to find authentic ways to lighten yet enrich. Spicy and aromatic, it's definitely a healthy alternative.

	Classic	Lighter
Kcals	613	402
Fat	34 g	12 g
Sat fat	20 g	3 g
Salt	0.42 g	0.35 g

Per serving 402 kcals

Protein 43 g, carbs 33 g, fat 12 g, sat fat 3 g, fibre 1 g, sugar 7 g, salt 0.35 g

Serves 4

Prep: 15 minutes
Cook: 45 minutes

2 tablespoons vegetable oil

2 medium onions, chopped

5 cardamom pods

3 garlic cloves, finely chopped

2.5 cm (1 inch) piece fresh root ginger, peeled and finely chopped

1 cinnamon stick

600 g (1 lb 5 oz) boneless, skinless chicken breasts, cut into bite-sized pieces

2 teaspoons ground coriander

1½ teaspoons garam masala

¼ teaspoon ground mace

¼ teaspoon ground black pepper

150 ml (¼ pint) natural yogurt, at room temperature

100 ml (3½ fl oz) full-fat milk

2 small green chillies, deseeded and shredded

handful of fresh coriander leaves and stems, coarsely chopped

1 tablespoon flaked almonds, toasted

salt

250 g (9 oz) basmati rice cooked, with a pinch of saffron threads, to serve

1 Heat 1 tablespoon of the oil in a deep sauté pan. Tip in the onions, then fry over a medium-high heat for about 12–15 minutes, stirring occasionally, until they are a rich golden colour. Meanwhile, make a slit down the length of each cardamom pod just deep enough to reveal the seeds. Remove the onions from the heat. Transfer a third of them to a mini blender along with the garlic, ginger and 2 tablespoons water. Whizz together to make a smooth paste. Set aside.

2 Return the onions in the pan to the heat, add the remaining oil, the cardamom pods and cinnamon stick, then stir-fry for 2 minutes. Stir in the chicken, ground coriander, 1¼ teaspoons of the garam masala, the mace and pepper, then stir-fry for another 2 minutes. Reserve 3 tablespoons of the yogurt, then slowly add the rest, 1 tablespoon at a time, stirring between each spoonful.

3 Stir the onion paste into the mixture and stir-fry for 2–3 minutes. Stir in 150 ml (¼ pint) water, then the milk. Bring to the boil, then simmer, covered, for 20 minutes, scattering in the chillies for the final 5 minutes. Remove the cardamom pods and cinnamon stick. The flavours mellow all the more if refrigerated overnight. When gently reheating, splash in a little water if needed to slacken the korma sauce.

4 Finish by stirring in the chopped fresh coriander. Taste and add a little salt if you wish. Swirl in the reserved yogurt. Spoon the korma into bowls, then scatter a few toasted almonds over each portion with a sprinkling of the remaining garam masala. Serve with the saffron rice on the side.

Replace cream or coconut milk with milk and yogurt to reduce fat

Lasagne

Traditionally, lasagne was made for special occasions and can be very rich. The pasta should be rolled out thinly to create fine layers – this speedier version has fewer layers of pasta for a similar light effect.

	Classic	Lighter
Kcals	770	447
Fat	50 g	19 g
Sat fat	26 g	9 g
Salt	1.99 g	0.96 g

Per serving 447 kcals

Protein 38 g, carbs 31 g, fat 19 g, sat fat 9 g, fibre 4 g, sugar 9 g, salt 0.96 g

Serves 6

Prep: 35–40 minutes
Cook: 1 hour 50 minutes

For the meat sauce

1 tablespoon olive oil

1 onion, chopped

2 medium carrots, diced

3 plump garlic cloves, finely chopped

250 g (9 oz) lean rump steak, trimmed of all fat, thinly sliced, then very finely chopped

250 g (9 oz) lean pork mince

100 ml (3½ fl oz) red wine

2 tablespoons tomato purée

400 g (14 oz) can plum tomatoes

½ teaspoon ground nutmeg, plus a pinch

handful of basil leaves, torn

For the other layers

300 g (11 oz) spinach leaves

1 medium egg

250 g (9 oz) ricotta cheese

handful of flat leaf parsley leaves, chopped

6 wide sheets (about 175 g/6 oz) no pre-cook lasagne

125 g (4 ½ oz) ball mozzarella, preferably buffalo, roughly chopped

50 g (2 oz) Parmesan cheese, coarsely grated

200 g (7 oz) cherry tomatoes on the vine

salt and freshly ground black pepper

basil leaves and green salad leaves, to serve

1 Make the meat sauce. Heat the oil in a large sauté pan, then add the onion and fry for 5 minutes until golden. Add the carrots and garlic and fry for 2 minutes more. Stir in both meats, breaking up the pork with a wooden spoon. Cook over a high heat until the meat is no longer pink and the juices are released. Pour in the wine, scrape the bottom of the pan as you stir, then cook for 1–2 minutes until the liquid is reduced.

2 Next add the tomato purée, tomatoes and 2 tablespoons water, then stir to break up tomatoes. Add ½ teaspoon nutmeg and some pepper, cover, then simmer for 1 hour, stirring occasionally. Taste, season with salt if necessary and stir in the torn basil. The sauce can be chilled for up to 1 day at this stage.

3 Meanwhile, prepare the other layers. Tip the spinach into a large bowl and pour over boiling water. After 30 seconds, tip the spinach into a colander and put under cold running water briefly to cool. Squeeze to remove excess water. Beat the egg in a bowl, then mix with the ricotta, parsley, the pinch of nutmeg and pepper.

4 Soak the lasagne sheets in a single layer in boiling water for 5 minutes. (Although the packet says no pre-cook, I find soaking improves the texture.) Drain well. Preheat the oven to 200°C (fan 180°C /400°F/gas mark 6).

5 Spread a few big spoonfuls of sauce to barely cover the base of a 20 x 28 cm (8 x 11 inches) ovenproof dish. Cover with 2 sheets of lasagne, then spread over half the remaining sauce. Cover with 2 more lasagne sheets, then scatter the spinach evenly over. Spread the ricotta mixture on top and cover with 2 more lasagne sheets. Spread with the remaining sauce, then scatter over the mozzarella and Parmesan to almost cover the meat. Top with the cherry tomatoes and some pepper, then cover loosely with foil.

6 Bake for 35 minutes, then remove the foil and bake 5–10 minutes more. Leave for a few minutes, then scatter with basil and serve with salad.

OTHER WAYS TO USE...

The meat sauce
Serve as a Bolognese sauce over spaghetti or tagliatelle.

Replace beef mince with lean pork mince and rump steak and use less oil to reduce fat

•

Try ricotta instead of béchamel sauce

•

Use spinach as one of the lasagne layers

•

Boost veg by mixing carrots into a meat sauce and topping with tomatoes

Pork stir-fry

Perfect for when there's just the two of you, a stir-fry is one of the fastest suppers to cook. Choosing the cut of meat wisely helps lower the fat – but there can still be a danger from it being high in salt if too much soy sauce is splashed in. I've found several ways to trim the fat and salt, so they have been dramatically reduced, but you won't miss out on flavour.

	Classic	Lighter
Kcals	348	230
Fat	22.7 g	8.8 g
Sat fat	6.5 g	1.8 g
Salt	4.1 g	1.3 g

Per serving 230 kcals

Protein 31.8 g, carbs 6 g, fat 8.8 g, sat fat 1.8 g, fibre 3.4 g, sugar 2.9 g, salt 1.3 g

Serves 2

Prep: 25 minutes
Cook: 10 minutes

1 teaspoon rice wine or dry sherry

1 tablespoon dark soy sauce

½ teaspoon Chinese five-spice powder

1 teaspoon cornflour

250 g (9 oz) fillet of pork, trimmed of all fat, cut into thin, 5–7.5 cm (2–3 inch) long slices

5 spring onions, ends trimmed

6 asparagus spears, trimmed

100 g (4 oz) pak choi

85 g (3 oz) tenderstem broccoli spears

1 teaspoon groundnut oil

2 teaspoons finely chopped fresh root ginger

2 garlic cloves, finely chopped

½ teaspoon sesame oil

1 teaspoon toasted sesame seeds

freshly ground black pepper

1 Mix together the rice wine or sherry, soy sauce, five-spice, cornflour and a grinding of pepper in a shallow dish. Toss in the pork to coat it, cover and leave to marinate while you prepare the vegetables.

2 Slice the spring onions and asparagus diagonally into 5 cm (2 inch) pieces. Slice the pak choi into 2.5 cm (1 inch) pieces and the broccoli spears into 5 cm (2 inch) pieces. Steam the asparagus and broccoli for 2 minutes, lay the pak choi on top and steam for another 1–1½ minutes so that it still has a bit of bite to it. Remove from the steamer.

3 Heat a wok or large frying pan, preferably non-stick. Pour in the groundnut oil and, when it is hot, add the pork and stir-fry for 2 minutes or until almost cooked and turning brown. Drop in the spring onions, ginger and garlic and stir-fry for another 2 minutes. Stir in enough water to make it a bit saucy, about 125 ml (4 fl oz), then mix in the steamed vegetables to quickly warm through. For more sauce, pour in a splash more water. Serve drizzled with the sesame oil and sprinkled with the sesame seeds.

Reduce salt greatly by using less soy sauce and adding five-spice powder to maintain flavour, use dark soy sauce for a more intense taste and bulk it out with water

Steak and kidney pie

Everyone enjoys the meat and gravy in this dish and the pastry needs to be generous and gusty, so this is a healthier pie that is still rich, desirable and hearty.

	Classic	Lighter
Kcals	683	373
Fat	41 g	14 g
Sat fat	22 g	5 g
Salt	1.22 g	0.42 g

Per serving 373 kcals

Protein 33 g, carbs 28 g, fat 14 g, sat fat 5 g, fibre 3 g, sugar 7 g, salt 0.42 g

Serves 6

Prep: 30 minutes
Cook: 2¼ hours

For the filling

200 g (7 oz) lamb's kidneys, halved

1 tablespoon rapeseed oil

2 onions, chopped

2 bay leaves

4 sprigs of thyme

600 g (1 lb 5 oz) lean stewing steak, cut into chunks

100 ml (3½ fl oz) red wine

2 teaspoons tomato purée

1 teaspoon English mustard powder

2 tablespoons plain flour

1 large carrot, chopped

4 flat mushrooms, thickly sliced

175 g (6 oz) chestnut mushrooms, quartered or halved if small

3 tablespoons chopped parsley

For the pastry

140 g (5 oz) plain flour, plus extra for dusting

1 teaspoon thyme leaves (optional)

25 g (1 oz) very cold (or frozen) butter

4 tablespoons 2% fat Greek yogurt

2 tablespoons extra virgin olive oil

salt and freshly ground black pepper

1 Cut out and discard the thin tubes from the kidneys. Rinse the kidneys in cold water until the water runs clear, pat dry, then chop them into small pieces. Heat the oil in a large saucepan or deep sauté pan. Add the onions, bay leaves and sprigs of thyme and fry over a medium heat for 8–10 minutes until the onions are really golden, stirring often. Fill the kettle and put it on.

2 Add the steak and kidney to the pan and stir-fry briefly, just until they lose their pink colour. Turn up the heat, pour in the wine and stir to deglaze the bottom of the pan, then let it boil over a high heat for 2–3 minutes until reduced and absorbed into the meat. Stir in the tomato purée and mustard powder. Sift in the flour, stirring, then stir for a couple of minutes.

3 Pour in 400 ml (14 fl oz) boiling water and continue stirring until the mixture starts to boil and is thickened. Tip in the carrot and both mushrooms, reduce the heat and cover with a lid, then leave to simmer gently for about 1 hour, stirring occasionally. Remove the lid and simmer for another 25–30 minutes or until the meat is very tender and the gravy has thickened slightly.

4 Take the pan off the heat and remove the bay leaves and sprigs of thyme. Stir in the parsley, season to taste, then transfer to a 23 cm (9 inch) round pie or ovenproof dish and leave to cool slightly. Preheat the oven to 200°C (fan 180°C/400°F/gas mark 6).

5 While the meat is cooling, make the pastry. Put the flour, and thyme, if using, into a bowl. Grate in the cold or frozen butter, make a well in the centre, then add the yogurt, olive oil, a pinch of salt and a good grinding of black pepper. Using a table knife, mix together with 2 teaspoons cold water, then gently gather together with your hands to form a dough. Remove from the bowl and knead briefly until smooth.

6 Roll out the pastry on a lightly floured surface until it's slightly bigger than the top of the pie dish. Lay the pastry over the meat and trim the edges so that it slightly overhangs the edges of the dish. Make 2 small slits in the centre. Flute the edges, then roll out the trimmings and cut out 6 diamond-shaped leaves. Dampen one side and lay them on the pastry lid. Place the dish on a baking sheet, then bake in the oven for about 25 minutes or until the pastry is golden.

use lean stewing steak – and less of it – to lower fat

•

make a shortcrust pastry with minimum butter, adding olive oil and yogurt instead

•

use water instead of stock for gravy and bump up the flavour with herbs, wine, tomato purée and mustard powder to reduce salt

•

increase veg by adding mushrooms and carrots

Crispy chicken

If you love takeaway chicken, you will be amazed by this low-fat version. The chicken is only fried briefly and then cooked in the oven, greatly reducing the amount of fat. The longer you leave the chicken pieces in the buttermilk marinade, the more tender and juicy they will be. The crispy chicken pieces are delicious served with crunchy coleslaw.

	Classic	Lighter
Kcals	412	319
Fat	22.7 g	10.5 g
Sat fat	6 g	1.1 g
Salt	3.5 g	0.7 g

Per serving 319 kcals

Protein 37.1 g, carbs 18.6 g, fat 10.5 g, sat fat 1.1 g, fibre 0.8 g, sugar 2.2 g, salt 0.7 g

Serves 4

Prep: 15 minutes, plus marinating
Cook: 25 minutes

150 ml (¼ pint) buttermilk

2 plump garlic cloves, crushed

4 boneless, skinless chicken breasts, total weight 550 g (1 lb 4 oz)

50 g (2 oz) Japanese panko breadcrumbs

2 tablespoons self-raising flour

½ rounded teaspoon paprika

¼ rounded teaspoon English mustard powder

¼ rounded teaspoon dried thyme

¼ teaspoon hot chilli powder

½ teaspoon ground black pepper

pinch of fine sea salt

3 tablespoons rapeseed oil

Crunchy Coleslaw (see p.63), to serve

1 To prepare the marinade, pour the buttermilk into a wide, shallow dish and stir in the garlic. Slice the chicken into chunky slices, about 9.5 cm (3¾ inches) long x 3–4 cm (1¼–1½ inches) wide. Lay the chicken in the dish and turn it over in the buttermilk so that it is well coated. Cover and leave in the fridge for 1–2 hours, or preferably overnight.

2 To prepare the coating for the chicken, heat a large, non-stick frying pan and tip in the panko crumbs and flour. Toast them in the pan for 2–3 minutes, stirring regularly so that they brown evenly and don't burn. Tip the crumb mix into a bowl and stir in the paprika, mustard, thyme, chilli powder, pepper and sea salt. Set aside.

3 When you are ready to cook the chicken, preheat the oven to 230°C (fan 210°C/450°F/gas mark 8). Line a baking tin with foil and sit a wire rack (preferably non-stick) on top. Transfer half the crumb mix to a medium-large plastic bag. Lift half the chicken from the buttermilk, leaving the marinade clinging to it. Transfer it to the bag of seasoned crumbs. Seal the end of the bag and give it a good shake so that the chicken gets well covered (you could do all the crumbs and chicken together if you prefer, but it's easier to coat it evenly in 2 batches).

4 Remove the chicken from the bag. Heat 1 tablespoon of the oil in a large, non-stick frying pan, then add the chicken pieces and fry for 1½ minutes without moving them. Turn the chicken over, pour in another ½ tablespoon of the oil to cover the base of the pan and fry for 1 minute more, so that both sides are becoming golden. Using tongs, transfer to the wire rack. Repeat with the remaining seasoned crumbs, oil and chicken.

5 Bake all the chicken on the rack for 15 minutes until cooked and crisp. Serve with Crunchy Coleslaw (see opposite).

To provide a low-fat coating for the crumb mix
to stick to, use buttermilk

•

Use Panko breadcrumbs – Japanese dried bread flakes.
When fried, they absorb less fat than regular breadcrumbs
and stay light and crisp once cooked

Crunchy coleslaw

Coleslaw salad is a traditional accompaniment to takeaway fried chicken, but usually not much better for you. This version still has creaminess and crunch, but without all the mayonnaise.

	Classic	Lighter
Kcals	189	123
Fat	17.3 g	7.2 g
Sat fat	2.6 g	1.6 g
Salt	1.5 g	0.4 g

Per serving 123 kcals

Protein 4.1 g, carbs 10.1 g, fat 7.2 g, sat fat 1.6 g, fibre 4.7 g, sugar 8.7 g, salt 0.4 g

Serves 4

Prep: 20 minutes, plus chilling and standing (optional)

½ small white cabbage, 300 g (11 oz) total weight

2 carrots, coarsley grated, 175 g (6 oz) total weight

6 spring onions, ends trimmed and chopped

2 teaspoons rapeseed oil

2 teaspoons white wine vinegar

2 teaspoons wholegrain mustard

2 tablespoons natural yogurt

2 tablespoons half-fat crème fraîche

2 tablespoons orange juice

2 tablespoons sunflower seeds, toasted

salt and freshly ground black pepper

1 To make the coleslaw, cut out and discard the hard core from the cabbage, then finely shred it. Place it in a bowl with the carrots and spring onions and mix well. Season with pepper and a pinch of salt, then cover and chill for 1–2 hours (optional).

2 Mix together the oil, vinegar and mustard in a small bowl, then stir in the yogurt, crème fraîche and orange juice. Set aside.

3 When ready to serve, pour the dressing over the veggies, add the sunflower seeds and toss together. Let the coleslaw sit for 10–15 minutes to allow the flavours to blend.

Toasting seeds and adding mustard to the coleslaw dressing gives extra flavour, so you need less salt

Macaroni cheese

Making macaroni cheese is a bit of a juggling act, so it's easier if you get a few things prepared ahead. I've found new ways to lighten this dish so it has half the fat but all the flavour.

	Classic	Lighter
Kcals	821	503
Fat	43 g	19 g
Sat fat	26 g	11 g
Salt	1.98 g	1.15 g

Per serving 503 kcals

Protein 26 g, carbs 62 g, fat 19 g, sat fat 11 g, fibre 3 g, sugar 14 g, salt 1.15 g.

Serves 4

Prep: 30 minutes
Cook: 35 minutes

550 ml (19 fl oz) semi-skimmed milk

25 g (1 oz) cornflour

1 heaped teaspoon English mustard powder

1 large garlic clove, finely chopped

generous pinch of crushed dried chillies

140 g (5 oz) extra mature Cheddar cheese, such as Davidstow or Denhay

25 g (1 oz) Parmesan cheese

25 g (1 oz) fresh breadcrumbs

450 g (1 lb) mix of tomatoes, such as cherry and medium vine

1 bunch spring onions, ends trimmed

200 g (7 oz) macaroni

150 ml (¼ pint) buttermilk

salt and freshly ground black pepper

1 Mix 3 tablespoons of the milk with the cornflour and mustard, and set aside. Heat the rest of the milk with the garlic until just coming to the boil. Remove from the heat, sprinkle in the crushed chillies and leave to infuse while you get everything else ready.

2 Coarsely grate both cheeses, keeping them separate. Mix a handful of the Cheddar into the breadcrumbs with a grinding of pepper. Thickly slice the medium tomatoes and halve the cherry. Finely slice the spring onions. Preheat the oven to 190°C (fan 170°C/375°F/gas mark 5).

3 Bring a pan of water up to the boil, tip in the macaroni, give it a stir so that it doesn't stick and then cook for 6 minutes, stirring occasionally. Stir in the spring onions and cook for another 2 minutes. Meanwhile, make the sauce. Stir the cornflour mix into the warm milk. Return the pan to the heat, then bring to the boil, stirring, until thickened and smooth. Remove from the heat and stir in the Parmesan, most of the remaining Cheddar and some pepper to taste. Stir in the buttermilk.

4 Tip the macaroni into a colander, drain, then hold under a very hot tap to keep it all separate. Drain well, then stir into the sauce. Pour into an ovenproof dish, about 30 x 20 cm (12 x 8 inches). Lay the tomatoes over the top, then scatter over the cheesy breadcrumbs, the rest of the cheese and a grating of pepper. Bake for about 15 minutes until starting to bubble around the edges. Grill for about 5 minutes until the top is crisp and well browned. Let sit for a few minutes to settle before serving.

Reduce the fat by making a butterless sauce, using less of an extra mature cheese combined with Parmesan to maintain flavour, and substituting some of the milk for ultra-low-fat buttermilk

Chicken pie

It's hard to resist the temptation of a classic chicken pie with its creamy filling and crisp, buttery shortcrust or puff pastry topping. This recipe has rich, comforting qualities also – but in a much healthier way.

	Classic	Lighter
Kcals	794	320
Fat	51.3 g	10.4 g
Sat fat	29.3 g	3.6 g
Salt	2.15 g	1.37 g

Per serving 320 kcals

Protein 34 g, carbs 22 g, fat 10 g, sat fat 4 g, fibre 3g, sugar 7 g, salt 1.37 g

Serves 4

Prep: 30 minutes, plus cooling
Cook: 45–50 minutes

For the filling

450 ml (16 fl oz) chicken stock, from a cube

100 ml (3½ fl oz) dry white wine

2 garlic cloves, finely chopped

3 sprigs of thyme

1 sprig tarragon, plus 1 tablespoon chopped tarragon leaves

225 g (8 oz) carrots, cut into batons

4 boneless, skinless chicken breasts, 500 g (1 lb 2 oz) total weight

225 g (8 oz) leeks, trimmed, cleaned and sliced

2 tablespoons cornflour mixed with 2 tablespoons water

3 tablespoons crème fraîche

1 heaped teaspoon Dijon mustard

1 heaped tablespoon chopped flat leaf or curly parsley

For the topping

3 sheets filo pastry, each approximately 38 x 30 cm (15 x 12 inches), about 70 g (2½ oz) total weight

1 tablespoon rapeseed oil

freshly ground black pepper

1 Pour the stock and wine into a large, wide frying pan. Add the garlic, thyme, tarragon sprig and carrots, bring to the boil, then lower the heat and simmer for 3 minutes. Lay the chicken in the stock, grind over some pepper, cover and simmer for 5 minutes. Scatter the leek slices over the chicken, cover again, then gently simmer for 10 more minutes, so that the leeks can steam while the chicken cooks. Remove from the heat and let the chicken sit in the stock for about 15 minutes to keep it moist while cooling slightly.

2 Strain the stock into a jug – you should have 500 ml (18 fl oz); if not, make up with water. Tip the chicken and vegetables into a 1.5 litre (2¾ pint) pie dish and discard the herb sprigs.

3 Pour the stock back into the frying pan, then slowly pour in the cornflour mixture. Return the pan to the heat and bring to the boil, stirring constantly, until thickened. Remove from the heat and stir in the crème fraîche, mustard, chopped tarragon and parsley. Season with pepper. Preheat the oven to 200°C (fan 180°C/400°F/gas mark 6).

4 Tear or cut the chicken into chunky shreds. Pour the sauce over the chicken mixture, then stir everything together.

5 Cut each sheet of filo into 4 squares or rectangles. Layer them on top of the filling, brushing each sheet with some of the oil as you go. Lightly scrunch up the filo so that it doesn't lie completely flat and tuck the edges into the sides of the dish, or lay them on the edges if the dish has a rim. Grind over a little pepper, place the dish on a baking sheet, then bake for 20–25 minutes until the pastry is golden and the sauce is bubbling. Serve immediately.

OTHER WAYS TO USE...

The filling
Serve minus the pastry lid with boiled rice instead, or toss with cooked pasta for a family-friendly supper.

The filo pastry topping
Use to cover a fish pie, or apple or other fruit pie, instead of high-fat puff or shortcrust pastry.

use skinless chicken breasts rather than thighs to reduce fat

•

Boost flavour by poaching chicken in stock and a little wine, with some garlic and herbs

•

Pack in as many vegetables as possible

•

Blend cornflour into the flavoured stock to make and thicken the sauce. For a rich creaminess, replace double cream with some crème fraîche

Shepherd's pie

Shepherd's pie uses lamb mince rather than beef or pork, which means it is slightly higher in fat, so this recipe uses the leanest I could find. Substituting some of the meat for lentils really transforms this recipe.

	Classic	Lighter
Kcals	666	429
Fat	38 g	12 g
Sat fat	20 g	4 g
Salt	1 g	0.91 g

Per serving 429 kcals

Protein 22 g, carbs 63 g, fat 12 g, sat fat 4 g, fibre 11 g, sugar 15 g, salt 0.91 g

Serves 4

Prep: 25 minutes
Cook: 1 hour 25–30 minutes

For the filling

1 tablespoon rapeseed oil

1 onion, chopped

3–4 sprigs of thyme

2 carrots, diced, about 300 g (11 oz) total weight

250 g (9 oz) 10% fat lamb mince

1 tablespoon plain flour

1 teaspoon vegetable bouillon, made up to 350 ml (12 fl oz) stock with boiling water

225g (8 oz) can chopped tomatoes

1 tablespoon tomato purée

400 g (14 oz) can green lentils with no added salt, drained

1 teaspoon Worcestershire sauce

For the topping

650 g (1 lb 7 oz) potatoes, King Edward or Maris Piper, roughly chopped

250 g (9 oz) sweet potatoes, roughly chopped

2 tablespoons half-fat crème fraîche

1 tablespoon semi-skimmed milk

freshly ground black pepper

1 Heat the oil in a large, deep sauté pan or saucepan. Tip in the onion and sprigs of thyme and fry for 2–3 minutes. Then add the carrots and fry together for 5–8 minutes, stirring occasionally until the vegetables start to brown. Stir in the mince to break it down. Fry for 1–2 minutes until no longer pink. Stir in the flour, scraping the bottom of the pan in case the meat sticks, then cook for another 1–2 minutes. Pour in the stock and stir until thickened. Stir in the tomatoes, tomato purée, lentils and Worcestershire sauce and season with pepper. Reduce the heat and simmer, covered, for 45 minutes, stirring occasionally.

2 Meanwhile, prepare the topping. Place all the chopped potatoes into a large pan of boiling water. Bring back to the boil, then simmer for 12–15 minutes or until the potatoes are tender. Drain well in a colander, then tip back into the pan. Mash with a masher or, briefly, with an electric hand mixer until smooth. Beat in the crème fraîche and milk with a wooden spoon until light and fluffy. Preheat the oven to 200°C (fan 180°C/400°F/gas mark 6).

3 Spoon the meat into a 1.5 litre (2¾ pint) pie dish and remove the sprigs of thyme. Top with the mash and smooth over with a knife. Use a fork to create a ridged pattern on top. Place the dish on a baking sheet and bake for about 20–25 minutes until piping hot and the filling starts to bubble around the edges. If the top is not brown enough, pop it under a hot grill for 5 minutes or so until the mash is crisp and golden. Let it sit for 5 minutes, then serve.

use lean mince to reduce fat and rapeseed oil to reduce saturated fat

Pizza Margherita

As with many things that have a bread base, it's what you scatter on to a pizza that can pile on the fat, especially saturated fat. Even with the simple, classic Margherita, the main fat culprit is cheese. With less kneading required (thanks to a method food writer Dan Lepard showed me) and a few easy tweaks, this pizza is lower in fat and salt, but still big on flavour.

	Classic	Lighter
Kcals	601	498
Fat	23.3 g	13.5 g
Sat fat	12 g	6.6 g
Salt	2.8 g	1.7 g

Per serving 498 kcals

Protein 19.6 g, carbs 73.7 g, fat 13.5 g, sat fat 6.6 g, fibre 3.9 g, sugar 5.6 g, salt 1.7 g

Makes 2 (each pizza serves 2)

Prep: 20 minutes, plus rising and resting
Cook: 15 minutes per pizza

For the dough

350 g (12 oz) strong white flour, plus extra for dusting

25 g (1 oz) semolina, preferably coarse, plus 1 teaspoon

1 teaspoon salt

7 g sachet fast-action (also called easy-blend) dried yeast

3 teaspoons olive oil

For the topping

400 g (14 oz) can plum tomatoes

3 garlic cloves, finely chopped

1 tablespoon tomato purée

2 handfuls basil leaves

50 g (2 oz) mozzarella cheese

200 g(7 oz) ricotta cheese

200 g (7 oz) cherry tomatoes, halved

25 g (1 oz) rocket leaves

2 tablespoons grated Parmesan cheese

salt and freshly ground black pepper

1 Combine the flour, the 25 g (1 oz) semolina, salt and yeast in a large mixing bowl. Pour in 2 teaspoons of the oil and nearly all of the 275 ml (9½ fl oz)water and mix together with your hands, adding the rest of the water to pick up any dry bits in the bottom of the bowl if needed. The dough should feel very sticky. Once it is mixed, cover and leave for 15 minutes.

2 Transfer the dough to a very lightly floured surface and knead for just 12 times. Shape it into a ball and return it to the bowl. Cover and leave for 10 minutes. Repeat the kneading and leaving for 10 minutes. Then, knead one more time and leave for 15 minutes.

3 While the dough is resting, prepare the topping. Tip the can of tomatoes into a sieve set over a bowl to drain off the juices. Put the tomatoes in a bowl and snip them into small pieces using scissors. Stir in the garlic and tomato purée with some pepper and a pinch of salt. Set aside. Line a baking sheet with baking parchment and sprinkle with ½ teaspoon of the remaining semolina. Preheat the oven to 240°C (fan 220°C/475°F/gas mark 9).

4 Cut the dough in half. Keep one half in the bowl and knead the other half just a few times on a lightly floured surface. Roll out to a 28 cm (11 inch) circle, pulling it into shape as well as rolling if that is easier. If the dough is sticking while rolling out, rub just a little of the remaining oil on the work surface to help it grip. Lift it on to the baking sheet, draped over a rolling pin if that works better.

5 Spread half of the tomato sauce over the dough, almost to the edge. Scatter over one handful of the basil in torn pieces. Tear half of the mozzarella and scatter that over, then dot small spoonfuls of the ricotta all over the dough. Scatter over half of the cherry tomatoes and season with pepper. Bake for 15 minutes until the dough is golden and crisp and the topping is bubbling. Repeat with the other half of the dough and toppings. Serve each pizza scattered with half of the rocket and Parmesan with a drizzle of the remaining oil over each (about ½ teaspoon over each).

TIPS

- Salt has been slightly reduced in the dough, but it's worth noting that if you reduce it too much, your dough will be less lively, as a certain amount is necessary to create a good texture and stop it from being slack.

- Semolina is added to give the dough authenticity and to enrich and strengthen it.

- If you wish to increase the fibre in the dough, replace 100 g (4 oz) of the strong white flour with strong wholemeal flour.

Make a no-cook tomato base, to eliminate oil for cooking

•

Scatter extra fresh tomatoes and rocket on top to add to your five a day

•

Lower the fat by replacing some of the mozzarella with ricotta cheese

•

Bake on a baking sheet lined with baking parchment, so there's no need to oil it

Burgers with roasted pepper salsa

Burgers can be high in fat and calories, but it's not just the meat that's to blame. It's the little extras we like to pile on – like the cheese, ketchup and mayonnaise. This recipe lightens the load but not the burger experience.

	Classic	Lighter
Kcals	604	405
Fat	39.7 g	15.4 g
Sat fat	12.7 g	5 g
Salt	2 g	1.44 g

Per serving 405 kcals

Protein 32 g, carbs 37 g, fat 15.4 g, sat fat 5 g, fibre 5 g, sugar 10 g, salt 1.44 g

Serves 4

Prep: 25 minutes, plus chilling and cooling
Cook: 45–50 minutes

For the burgers

400 g (14 oz) 10% fat beef mince

5 spring onions, ends trimmed and finely chopped

140 g (5 oz) carrot, finely grated

2 garlic cloves, finely chopped

2 teaspoons Dijon mustard

1 tablespoon chopped tarragon

1 medium egg, beaten

4 wholemeal bread rolls, split in half

1½ teaspoons rapeseed oil

25 g (1 oz) watercress

For the roasted pepper salsa

2 large red peppers, halved lengthways, cored and deseeded

100 g (4 oz) cherry or baby plum tomatoes, halved

2 teaspoons lime juice

2 teaspoons snipped chives

¼ very small red onion, thinly sliced

pinch of crushed dried chillies

salt and freshly ground black pepper

1 Tip the mince into a bowl with the spring onions, grated carrot, garlic, mustard, tarragon and egg. Mix well using a fork. Season with pepper and a pinch of salt, then divide the mixture equally into 4. Flatten each piece with your hands into a 10 cm (4 inch) round, about 2 cm (¾ inch) thick. Chill for about 30 minutes. Alternatively, the burgers can be made a day ahead: stack the burgers between pieces of greaseproof paper to stop them sticking, wrap in clingfilm, then chill until ready to cook.

2 Meanwhile, preheat the oven to 200°C (fan 180°C/400°F/gas mark 6). Lay the peppers, cut-sides down, on a non-stick baking sheet. Roast for 35 minutes until the skins are charred, laying the tomatoes next to them, cut-side up, for the final 3 minutes just to soften slightly. Remove and immediately transfer the peppers to a small bowl, then cover with clingfilm. Leave for 5–10 minutes until cool enough to handle.

3 To make the salsa, peel off the pepper skins, chop the peppers and tip them back into the bowl to join any juices there. Chop the tomatoes and stir into the peppers with the lime juice, chives, onion and crushed chillies. Taste and season with pepper if necessary. Set aside. The salsa can be made 1–2 days ahead and chilled.

4   Heat a griddle pan, or cook the burgers on the barbecue. Lay the cut sides of the buns on the griddle and cook until marked with the griddle bars. Brush each burger on one side with some of the rapeseed oil. Place on the hot griddle, oiled-side down. Cook – don't move them or they may stick – for 5 minutes for medium, brush the unoiled side with the rest of the oil, then turn and cook for another 5 minutes. (For well done, add an extra 1–2 minutes to each side.)

5   Remove and let the burgers rest for 2–3 minutes. Drizzle a little of the pepper juices over the bottom of each bun to moisten, lay on some watercress sprigs and top with a burger, then a spoonful of the salsa, spooning over some more of the juices. Sandwich together with the tops of the buns.

OTHER WAYS TO USE...

The meat mix
Shape into meatballs and serve with spaghetti and a tomato sauce. Or omit the mustard and tarragon, replace with 1 tablespoon each chopped mint and oregano and serve in pitta bread with tomato, cucumber and natural yogurt.

The salsa
Offer as an accompaniment to barbecued fish or chicken. Or serve as bruschetta, spooned on to slices of griddled, lightly oiled French bread.

Reduce fat by using lean mince and bulking the mixture out with grated carrot

•

Brush oil on to the burgers direct, rather than the pan, to keep oil to a minimum

•

Flavour with mustard, garlic and tarragon to reduce salt

•

Up veg and vitamin c by mixing carrots into the burger mix, use red peppers and tomatoes in the salsa and replace regular lettuce with watercress

Onion tart

This dish classically has a rich, buttery pastry, uses oil and butter for frying the onions in and lots of cream and eggs to hold it all together. To turn things round, I tried a scone-like base that is lower in fat.

	Classic	Lighter
Kcals	604	309
Fat	49.7 g	16.6 g
Sat fat	26.8 g	7.4 g
Salt	0.97 g	0.84 g

Per serving 309 kcals

Protein 9 g, carbs 33 g, fat 16.6 g, sat fat 7.4 g, fibre 2 g, sugar 8 g, salt 0.84 g

Serves 6

Prep: 25 minutes
Cook: 45–50 minutes

For the filling

2 large red onions, about 550 g (1 lb 4 oz) total weight, halved lengthways

2 tablespoons rapeseed oil

2 medium eggs

200 ml (7 fl oz) half-fat crème fraîche

1 teaspoon thyme leaves

1 teaspoon Dijon mustard

25 g (1 oz) Gruyère cheese, grated

For the base

175 g (6 oz) self-raising flour, plus extra for dusting

25 g (1 oz) cold butter, cut into small pieces

100 g (4 oz) natural yogurt

4 tablespoons semi-skimmed milk

salt and freshly ground black pepper

green salad, to serve

1 Slice the onions into small, thin, wedge-shaped pieces. Heat the rapeseed oil in a large, preferably non-stick sauté or deep frying pan. Stir in the onions and fry over a medium heat for about 20 minutes. Stir only occasionally so that they can cook fairly undisturbed and caramelize underneath. When done, they should be well caramelized and sticky.

2 Meanwhile, prepare the base. Preheat the oven to 190°C (fan 170°C/375°F/ gas mark 5) and put in a baking sheet. Put the flour and butter in a bowl with a pinch of salt and rub with your fingertips until it resembles rough crumbs. Mix the yogurt and milk together, pour into the flour mixture and work together briefly with a knife until the dough just comes together. Remove from the bowl and gently press together to form a ball. Do not overwork.

3 Roll the dough out thinly on a lightly floured surface and use to line a 23 cm (9 inch) round, 2.5 cm (1 inch) deep, loose-bottomed fluted flan tin, pressing it with your fingers into the flutes. If the dough is a little sticky, dust your fingers in some flour.

4 Beat the eggs in a medium bowl, then stir in the crème fraîche, thyme, mustard and seasoning. Spoon and spread half of the onions into the base, season with pepper, then scatter over half of the cheese. Pour the egg mixture over the top, then scatter over the rest of the onions and cheese. Sit the tin on the hot baking sheet and bake for 25–30 minutes until the base and filling are cooked. Remove and cool for about 10 minutes, then remove from the tin and serve while fresh and warm, with a green salad.

Instead of a rich shortcrust pastry, line a tart tin with a scone-type base, which requires less fat

Chicken tikka masala

Like many Indian recipes, tikka masala needs to be done with a degree of authenticity using a core of key ingredients including cream and butter. This recipe tastes rich enough while massively cutting the fat content.

	Classic	Lighter
Kcals	566	515
Fat	40 g	10 g
Sat fat	13 g	2 g
Salt	2.11 g	0.3 g

Per serving (with rice) 515 kcals

Protein 47 g, carbs 58 g, fat 10 g, sat fat 2 g, fibre 5 g, sugar 7 g, salt 0.3 g

Serves 4

Prep: 35 minutes, plus marinating and soaking
Cook: 35 minutes

For the marinade

5 cm (2 inch) piece fresh root ginger, peeled

4 plump garlic cloves, peeled

3 tablespoons natural yogurt

2 teaspoons lime juice

1 tablespoon finely chopped fresh coriander leaves

½ teaspoon garam masala

½ teaspoon paprika

¼ teaspoon turmeric

¼–½ teaspoon hot chilli powder

1 teaspoon cumin seeds

1 teaspoon coriander seeds

½ teaspoon fenugreek seeds

600 g (1 lb 5 oz) boneless, skinless chicken breasts, cut into 4 cm (1½ inch) chunks

For the sauce

2 tablespoons rapeseed oil

2 onions, halved lengthways and sliced into rough, thin wedges

½ teaspoon paprika

½ teaspoon turmeric

½ teaspoon garam masala

¼ teaspoon hot chilli powder (optional)

2 tablespoons tomato purée

2 tablespoons natural yogurt

For the rice

250 g (9 oz) basmati rice

200 g (7 oz) frozen peas

salt

fresh coriander leaves and lime wedges, to serve

1 For the marinade, finely grate the ginger and garlic (you should have 1 tablespoon of each), then mix them together. Put half of this mix into a medium bowl, then stir in the yogurt, lime juice, chopped coriander, garam masala, paprika, turmeric and chilli powder.

2 Heat a small, heavy-based dry frying pan, tip in the cumin, coriander and fenugreek seeds, then heat briefly until toasted and smelling fragrant (they will start to jump in the pan). Remove and grind to a powder using a pestle and mortar.

3 Stir half of the ground spices into the yogurt mix (save the rest for the sauce). Stir the chicken chunks into the spiced yogurt until well coated. Cover and leave to marinate for at least 30 minutes or overnight in the fridge. Meanwhile, soak 8 wooden skewers in cold water for at least 30 minutes.

4 While the chicken is marinating, make the sauce. Heat the oil in a large pan. Add the onions, then fry over a medium heat for about 10 minutes, stirring occasionally, until softened and turning brown. Stir in the remaining ginger and garlic, and stir-fry for 2 minutes.

5 Mix the paprika, turmeric, garam masala and chilli powder, if using, into the onions with the rest of the toasted, ground spices. Cook for 1 minute, stirring to scrape up the bits from the bottom of the pan. Stir in the tomato purée, then 150 ml (¼ pint) water. Cook for 1 minute. Carefully transfer to a blender or food processor. Process to a thick, fairly smooth sauce. Return to the pan, pour in another 150 ml (¼ pint) water, then set aside. The sauce can be made a day ahead. Soak the rice in cold water for up to 30 minutes.

6 Preheat the grill to high. Thread the chicken on to the drained soaked wooden skewers, then balance them across a baking tray lined with foil so that they are slightly raised over it. Grill for 12–15 minutes, turning often, until cooked through and slightly charred around the edges.

7 Meanwhile, drain the rice, then place it in a pan with 375 ml (13 fl oz) water. Bring to the boil, then cook over a low heat, covered, for 8 minutes. Remove from the heat but leave covered for 5 minutes. Cook the peas in boiling water for 3 minutes, then drain. Fluff up the rice with a fork, then toss in the peas.

8 When ready to serve, reheat the sauce, stirring in any juices from the cooked chicken and a little more water to thin if necessary (it should be quite thick). Remove from the heat, stir in the yogurt, then season with a pinch of salt. Serve the chicken skewers with the rice, a scattering of coriander leaves and lime wedges.

Eliminate cream and butter and use natural yogurt instead to reduce fat

•

Boost flavour by roasting some of the spices – and carefully balancing others – rather than adding salt

•

Use rapeseed oil to lower saturated fat

Chicken cacciatore

An Italian classic that means 'hunter's stew', this dish is often traditionally cooked with a whole, jointed chicken, pancetta and a good slug of olive oil. All delicious, but all help to increase the fat. With just a few small changes that don't affect the desired taste, fat and calories have been dramatically reduced.

	Classic	Lighter
Kcals	620	262
Fat	40.3 g	6.2 g
Sat fat	11.5 g	1.3 g
Salt	1.6 g	1 g

Per serving 262 kcals

Protein 38.7 g, carbs 6.9 g, fat 6.2 g, sat fat 1.3 g, fibre 2.7 g, sugar 5.2 g, salt 1.0g

Serves 4

Prep: 15 minutes
Cook: 50 minutes

1 tablespoon olive oil

3 slices prosciutto, trimmed of excess fat

1 medium onion, chopped

2 garlic cloves, finely chopped

2 sprigs of sage

2 sprigs of rosemary

4 boneless, skinless chicken breasts, 550 g (1 lb 4 oz) total weight, preferably organic

150 ml (¼ pint) dry white wine

400 g (14 oz) can plum tomatoes in natural juice

1 tablespoon tomato purée

225 g (8 oz) chestnut mushrooms, trimmed and quartered or halved if small

small handful of chopped flat leaf parsley

salt and freshly ground black pepper

1   Heat the oil in a large, non-stick frying or sauté pan. Tip in the prosciutto and fry for about 2 minutes until crisp. Remove with a slotted spoon, letting any fat drain back into the pan, and set aside. Put the onion, garlic and sage and rosemary sprigs in the pan and fry for 3–4 minutes until the onion is starting to soften.

2   Spread the onion out in the bottom of the pan to make a bed of it, then lay the chicken breasts on top, skinned-side down. Season with pepper and fry for 5 minutes over a medium heat, turning the chicken once, until starting to brown on both sides and the onion is caramelizing on the bottom of the pan. Raise the heat, give a quick stir and, when all is sizzling, pour in the wine and let it bubble for 2 minutes to reduce slightly.

3   Lower the heat back to medium, return the prosciutto to the pan, then stir in the tomatoes (breaking them up with your spoon), tomato purée and mushrooms. Pour 4–5 tablespoons water into the empty can of tomatoes, rinse it around and pour it into the frying pan. Cover and simmer for 30 minutes or until the chicken is cooked through, then cook, uncovered, for 5 more minutes so that the sauce can thicken slightly. Season with pepper and a pinch of salt and serve scattered with the parsley.

choose lean, skinless chicken breasts and swop prosciutto for fatty pancetta or bacon to reduce fat and saturated fat

LIGHT ENTERTAINING

Thai green chicken curry

Fresh and fragrant, real Thai curry has a carefully balanced mix of hot, sour, sweet and salty, with coconut milk an integral flavour. So this recipe focuses on how to achieve this using healthy ingredients and methods.

	Classic	Lighter
Kcals	817	487
Fat	44 g	16 g
Sat fat	32 g	10 g
Salt	2.78 g	0.96 g

Per serving (with rice) 487 kcals

Protein 35 g, carbs 55 g, fat 16 g, sat fat 10 g, fibre 2 g, sugar 4 g, salt 0.96 g

Serves 4

Prep: 35 minutes
Cook: 20 minutes

For the curry paste

20 g (¾ oz) bunch fresh coriander, stalks and leaves separated

2 shallots, finely chopped

1 lemon grass stalk, finely chopped

2 garlic cloves, finely chopped

1 cm (½ inch) piece fresh root ginger, peeled and finely chopped

3 small hot green chillies, finely chopped (include the seeds)

1 larger, mild-to-medium green chilli, finely chopped (include the seeds)

small handful of basil leaves

½ teaspoon ground cumin

½ teaspoon ground coriander

¼ teaspoon ground black pepper

1 teaspoon crumbled freeze-dried kaffir lime leaves

1 tablespoon lime juice

1 teaspoon sunflower oil

For the curry

1 tablespoon sunflower oil

400ml (14 fl oz) can reduced-fat coconut milk

3 boneless, skinless chicken breasts, about 450 g (1 lb) total weight, cut into bite-sized pieces

2 teaspoons fish sauce

½ teaspoon granulated palm or light muscovado sugar

4 freeze-dried kaffir lime leaves

100 g (4 oz) mangetout, thinly sliced lengthways

100 g (4 oz) green beans, stem ends trimmed and halved lengthways

finely shredded spring onions and lime wedges, to serve

For the rice

250 g (9 oz) Thai fragrant rice

1 For the curry paste, finely chop the coriander stalks and put them into a mini blender or small food processor with the shallots, lemon grass, garlic and ginger. Pulse until it is as smooth as you can get it. Add the chillies, basil, three-quarters of the coriander leaves, the ground cumin, coriander, pepper, lime leaves and lime juice, then pulse again. Mix in the oil and set aside. You will only need half of this paste; the rest can be chilled for a couple of days, or frozen for up to a month.

2 For the curry, heat the oil in a non-stick wok or deep sauté pan, stir in half of the curry paste, then stir-fry for 1 minute. Shake the coconut milk in its can, open, then pour two-thirds into the pan. Let it bubble away for 4–5 minutes, stirring now and then, until reduced and thickened slightly.

3 Cook the rice in a pan of boiling water, according to the packet instructions.

4 Meanwhile, add the chicken to the wok and stir-fry for 1–2 minutes until no longer pink. Stir in the fish sauce and sugar, then pour in the rest of the coconut milk to give a thinnish, creamy sauce. Lower the heat, add the lime leaves, then simmer for 5 minutes to gently finish cooking the chicken. The curry can be frozen at this point for up to 1 month.

5 While the chicken simmers, steam the mangetout and beans for a couple of minutes. Serve the curry in bowls with some of the vegetables piled on top (serve the rest separately) along with the spring onions and the rest of the coriander leaves. Accompany with a bowl of the cooked rice and lime wedges for squeezing over.

Replace coconut cream with reduced-fat coconut milk, cooking it to thicken and enrich

•

Reduce the amount of oil to reduce the fat further

•

Make your own curry paste to boost flavour and eliminate need for salt, as well as the need for using as much fish sauce and sugar

Chicken balti

Recipes for this vary enormously. Spices can be different and all too often, excess fat is used, which makes it very oily. This healthier version still has a bit of kick and is a lot better for you than a takeaway.

	Classic	Lighter
Kcals	309	217
Fat	15.4 g	6.6 g
Sat fat	6.1 g	1.3 g
Salt	0.9 g	0.5 g

Per serving 217 kcals

protein 30.2 g, carbs 10.2 g, fat 6.6 g, sat fat 1.3 g, fibre 2.5 g, sugar 8.2 g, salt 0.5 g

Serves 4

Prep: 25 minutes plus marinating
Cook: 30 minutes

450 g (1 lb) boneless, skinless chicken breasts, cut into bite-sized pieces

1 tablespoon lime juice

1 teaspoon paprika

¼ teaspoon hot chilli powder

1½ tablespoons sunflower or groundnut oil

1 cinnamon stick

3 cardamom pods, lightly bashed to split

1 small to medium green chilli

½ teaspoon cumin seeds

1 medium onion, coarsely grated

2 garlic cloves, very finely chopped

2.5 cm (1 inch) piece fresh root ginger, grated

½ teaspoon turmeric

1 teaspoon ground cumin

1 teaspoon ground coriander

1 teaspoon garam masala

250 ml (9 fl oz) passata

1 red pepper, cored, deseeded and cut into small chunks

1 medium tomato, chopped

85 g (3 oz) baby spinach leaves

handful of fresh coriander, chopped

salt and freshly ground black pepper

chapatis or basmati rice, to serve (optional)

Fry in a non-stick wok to reduce the fat for cooking

•

Stir in lots of vegetables to increase your five a day

1 Put the chicken in a non-metallic medium bowl. Mix in the lime juice, paprika, chilli powder and a grinding of black pepper, then cover and leave to marinate for at least 15 minutes, preferably a bit longer, in the fridge.

2 Heat 1 tablespoon of the oil in a large, non-stick wok or sauté pan. Tip in the cinnamon stick, cardamom pods, whole chilli and cumin seeds, and stir-fry briefly just to colour and release their fragrance. Stir in the onion, garlic and ginger and fry over a medium-high heat for 3–4 minutes until the onion starts to turn brown. Add the remaining oil, then drop in the chicken and stir-fry for 2–3 minutes or until it no longer looks raw. Mix the turmeric, cumin, ground coriander and garam masala together. Tip into the pan, lower the heat to medium and cook for 2 minutes. Pour in the passata and 150 ml (¼ pint) water, then drop in the chunks of pepper. When starting to bubble, lower the heat and simmer for 15–20 minutes or until the chicken is tender.

3 Stir in the tomato and simmer for 2–3 minutes, then add the spinach and turn it over in the pan to just wilt. Season with a little salt. If you want to thin down the sauce, splash in a little more water. Remove the cinnamon stick, chilli and cardamom pods, if you wish, before serving. Scatter with the fresh coriander and serve with warm chapatis or basmati rice, if you like.

Salmon en croûte

Salmon wrapped in crisp, buttery pastry is one of those entertaining dishes that is valuable to have in your repertoire. This version uses filo pastry to reduce the fat by half, and loses none of the wow factor.

	Classic	Lighter
Kcals	634	331
Fat	44.9 g	20.2 g
Sat fat	17.2 g	4.1 g
Salt	1.64 g	0.47 g

Per serving 331 kcals

Protein 26.6 g, carbs 11.6 g, fat 20.2 g, sat fat 4.1 g, fibre 1.1 g, sugar 1 g, salt 0.47 g

Serves 6

Prep: 30 minutes, plus cooling
Cook: 35 minutes

3 tablespoons olive oil

2 large shallots, finely chopped

140 g (5 oz) chestnut mushrooms, trimmed and finely chopped

3 garlic cloves, finely chopped

juice of ½ lemon

100 g (4 oz) watercress, chopped

2 tablespoons snipped dill

1 tablespoon snipped chives

2½ tablespoons half-fat crème fraîche

6 sheets filo pastry, each approximately 38 x 30 cm (15 x 12 inches), about 125 g (4½ oz) total weight

2 x skinned salmon fillets, about 350 g (12 oz) each

salt and freshly ground black pepper

1 Heat 2 tablespoons of the oil in a large, non-stick frying pan. Fry the shallots for 2–3 minutes to soften, then add the mushrooms and garlic and stir-fry over a high heat for another 3–4 minutes or until the mushrooms and shallots are golden and any liquid from the mushrooms has evaporated. Pour in the lemon juice – after a few seconds, that should have evaporated too. Remove from the heat, then stir in the watercress until it wilts. Stir in the dill and chives, and season with a little salt and pepper. Leave to cool.

2 Preheat the oven to 200°C (fan 180°C/400°F/gas mark 6). Line a baking sheet with baking parchment. When the mushroom mix is cool, stir in the crème fraîche. Lay one of the filo sheets on the work surface with the short end facing you. Brush all over with a little of the remaining oil. Layer up 4 more of the filo sheets in the same way, brushing each with a little of the oil.

3 Lay one of the salmon fillets, skin-side up, across the width of the filo, positioning it about one-third of the way up. Season it with pepper. Spoon and spread the cooled mushroom mix over the top of the fillet. Lay the other salmon fillet on top, skin-side down. Season again. Fold the short end of pastry nearest to you over the salmon, then bring the other end over to completely enclose the salmon, lifting it so that the join can tuck under it. Fold both pastry ends over as neatly as you can.

4 Brush the outside with a bit more of the remaining oil. Scrunch up the last sheet of filo, pressing it lightly on top in big folds, then carefully brush with the last of the oil. The dish can be prepared 3–4 hours ahead up to this point and chilled.

5 Transfer the salmon parcel to the baking sheet. Bake for 25 minutes until the pastry is crisp and golden. Check while it cooks, and if the top starts to brown too quickly, lay a sheet of foil very loosely over it. Remove from the oven and let the salmon sit for 2–3 minutes before slicing.

use a non-stick frying pan so that you can use less oil

•

Replace puff pastry with filo, to greatly reduce both fat and calories

•

include mushrooms to increase the levels of B vitamins, and watercress, also for its B vitamins as well as iron and minerals

•

use half-fat crème fraîche instead of double cream to reduce fat further

•

Glaze pastry with oil rather than egg

Spaghetti carbonara

It's one of the most popular pasta dishes, but with double cream, cheese, eggs and salty, fatty bacon in the original, this lighter version is sure to become a new favourite.

	Classic	Lighter
Kcals	935	527
Fat	49.8 g	16.1 g
Sat fat	21.9 g	6.3 g
Salt	3.73 g	1.63 g

Per serving 527 kcals

Protein 29.7 g, carbs 70 g, fat 16.1 g, sat fat 6.3 g, fibre 5.2 g, sugar 4.4 g, salt 1.63 g

Serves 4

Prep: 15 minutes
Cook: 20 minutes

2 large eggs

200 g (7 oz) frozen peas

350 g (12 oz) spaghetti

1 tablespoon olive oil

100 g (4 oz) lean back bacon, trimmed of excess fat, chopped into small pieces

2 plump garlic cloves, finely chopped

85 g (3 oz) Parmesan cheese, grated

salt and freshly ground black pepper

handful of snipped chives, to garnish

1 Bring a large saucepan of water to the boil with a pinch of salt. Beat the eggs in a bowl with a little pepper. Cook the peas in the boiling water for 2–3 minutes, drain, reserving the water, and set aside.

2 Return the pea cooking water to the pan, bring back to the boil and cook the spaghetti until al dente, following the packet instructions. While the spaghetti is cooking, heat the oil in a large, deep frying or sauté pan. Fry the bacon for several minutes until it starts to go crisp. Stir in the garlic and cook briefly until pale brown. Tip in the peas, and if the spaghetti isn't quite ready, keep it warm over a very low heat.

3 When the pasta is done, take the pan with the bacon in off the heat. Lift the spaghetti out of its pan with a pair of tongs (reserving the cooking water) and drop it into the frying pan with the garlic, bacon and peas. Mix most of the cheese into the eggs, keeping back a handful of cheese for sprinkling over each serving. Quickly pour in the eggs and cheese, lifting and stirring with the tongs so that everything mixes well and the spaghetti gets coated. Ladle in a little of the reserved pasta water, enough to coat the spaghetti and create a bit of sauce in the pan.

4 Spoon or twirl the pasta into shallow serving bowls using a long pronged fork. Serve immediately with a sprinkling of the reserved cheese, some snipped chives and a grinding of black pepper.

Eliminate cream and use the pasta water to create a sauciness

Nasi goreng

This is Indonesia's equivalent to China's popular fried rice, but when generous amounts of soy sauce are splashed in, it can quickly become high in salt. This recipe shows there are plenty of other ways to enhance flavour, trim the fat and still keep its unique taste.

	Classic	Lighter
Kcals	694	405
Fat	27.2 g	7.9 g
Sat fat	4.6 g	1.2 g
Salt	2.9 g	1.6 g

Per serving 405 kcals

Protein 30.7 g, carbs 50.9 g, fat 7.9g, sat fat 1.2 g, fibre 4.6 g, sugar 3.6 g, salt 1.6 g

Serves 4

Prep: 30 minutes
Cook: 20 minutes

140 g (5 oz) green beans, stem ends trimmed, quartered widthways

1 large egg

1 tablespoon semi-skimmed milk

generous pinch of turmeric

2 tablespoons rapeseed oil

225 g (8 oz) white long-grain rice

85 g (3 oz) fresh or frozen peas

3 shallots, finely chopped

2 garlic cloves, finely chopped

1 red Thai chilli, deseeded and finely chopped (or keep a few seeds in for extra heat)

2 boneless, skinless, chicken breasts, 300 g (11 oz) total weight, cut into 2.5 cm (1 inch) cubes

1 teaspoon paprika

1 teaspoon ground coriander

100 g (4 oz) cooked, peeled prawns

To serve

3 spring onions, ends trimmed

4 teaspoons dark soy sauce

50 g (2 oz) piece cucumber, diced

handful of chopped fresh coriander

lime wedges

salt and freshy ground black pepper

1 Steam (or boil) the beans for 4–5 minutes until tender-crisp. Drain if necessary, then run them under running cold water to stop them cooking further. Set aside.

2 Make an omelette. Beat the egg in a bowl, then mix in the milk and turmeric and some pepper. Pour 1 teaspoon of the oil into a large, non-stick frying pan. Pour in the egg and swirl the pan around so that the base is completely covered to give you a thin omelette about 23 cm (9 inches) in diameter. Cook over a medium heat for 1–2 minutes (there is no need to turn it over) until set on top and lightly browned underneath. Slide the omelette on to a board with the browned side underneath, roll it up tightly like a cigar, then cut across into thin slices. Set aside.

3 If you want to curl the spring onions for a garnish, halve each one, then slice into long, thin shreds. Put in a small bowl, cover with cold water and leave in the fridge to curl.

4 Cook the rice in a pan of boiling water for about 10 minutes or until just tender, adding the peas for the last 3 minutes.

5 While the rice is cooking, heat 1 tablespoon of the oil in a large sauté pan or wok, tip in the shallots, garlic and chilli and stir-fry for 2–3 minutes until softening and tinged brown. Pour in another 1 teaspoon of the oil, stir in the chicken and stir-fry for 4–5 minutes until cooked. Stir in the paprika, ground coriander, prawns and beans and cook for 1 more minute to heat everything through and cook the spices.

6 Drain the rice in a colander, and if you are still frying the chicken, sit the colander over a saucepan with a little gently boiling water in the bottom and cover the rice with the lid so that it can dry off slightly and keep warm in the steam.

7 Mix the cooked rice and sliced omelette into the chicken and gently stir to reheat well. Season with pepper and just a little salt. Serve each portion drizzled with a little of the rest of the oil and 1 teaspoon of the soy sauce, then scatter over some cucumber and chopped coriander and top with a small pile of the drained, shredded spring onions.

TIP

- Traditionally, this dish is made as a way of using up left-over cooked rice. Here it is cooked fresh to make it an instant meal, but if you do use left-over rice, it is important to cool it quickly after initial cooking, keep it in the fridge until ready to use, then reheat thoroughly before serving.

Lower fat and saturated fat by using lean, skinless chicken breast

•

Reduce fat further by frying in a non-stick pan and using less egg but extending it with some semi-skimmed milk

•

Lower salt by using fewer prawns and less soy sauce. Keep flavour up with extra spices and drizzle dark soy sauce over at the end for a direct taste hit

•

Include green beans and peas to improve your five a day and fibre content

Coq au vin

A rich and satisfying dish, ideal for winter entertaining. Best of all, this lighter version comes with the same deep flavour, but the fat and calories are greatly reduced. Keep the whole meal lighter and serve with Braised leeks and peas (see p. 202) and Creamy mash (see p. 213).

	Classic	Lighter
Kcals	818	420
Fat	53.8 g	13.2 g
Sat fat	18.1 g	3.2 g
Salt	1.2 g	1.4 g

Per serving 420 kcals

Protein 46.9 g, carbs 7.3 g, fat 13.2 g, sat fat 3.2 g, fibre 1.3 g, sugar 1.7 g, salt 1.4 g

Serves 6

Prep: 25 minutes
Cook: 1 hour 15–35 minutes

3 sprigs of thyme

2 sprigs of rosemary

2 bay leaves

3 tablespoons olive oil

100 g (4 oz) dry-cured smoked back bacon, trimmed of excess fat, chopped

12 small shallots, peeled

2 chicken legs. about 450 g (1 lb) total weight, skin removed

4 chicken thighs with bone and skin, about 650 g (1 lb 7 oz) total weight, skin removed

2 boneless, skinless chicken breasts, about 300 g (11 oz) total weight

3 garlic cloves, finely chopped

3 tablespoons brandy

600 ml (1 pint) red wine

150 ml (¼ pint) good-quality chicken stock

2 teaspoons tomato purée

250 g (9 oz) chestnut mushrooms, trimmed and halved if large

For the thickening paste

2 tablespoons plain flour

1½ teaspoons olive oil

1 teaspoon softened butter

salt and freshly ground black pepper

small handful of chopped flat leaf parsley, to garnish

1 Tie the herbs together to make a bouquet garni.

2 Heat 1 tablespoon of the oil in a large, heavy-based saucepan or flameproof casserole. Tip in the bacon and fry until crisp. Remove and drain on kitchen paper. Add the shallots to the pan and fry, stirring or shaking the pan often, for 5–8 minutes until well browned all over. Remove and set aside with the bacon.

3 Pat the chicken pieces dry with kitchen paper. Pour ½ tablespoon of the remaining oil into the pan, then fry half the chicken pieces, turning regularly, for 5–8 minutes until well browned. Remove, then repeat with the remaining chicken. Remove and set aside.

4 Scatter in the garlic and fry briefly, then, with the heat medium-high, pour in the brandy, stirring the bottom of the pan to deglaze. The alcohol should sizzle and start to evaporate so there is not much left.

5 Return the chicken legs and thighs to the pan along with any juices, then pour in a little of the wine, stirring the bottom of the pan again. Stir in the rest of the wine, the stock and tomato purée, drop in the bouquet garni, season with pepper and a pinch of salt, then return the bacon and shallots to the pan. Cover, lower the heat to a gentle simmer, add the chicken breasts and cook for 50 minutes–1 hour.

6 Just before serving, heat the remaining oil in a large, non-stick frying pan. Add the mushrooms and fry over a high heat for a few minutes until golden. Remove and keep warm.

7 Lift the chicken, shallots and bacon from the pan and transfer to a warmed serving dish. Remove the bouquet garni.

8 For the thickening paste, mix the flour, olive oil and butter in a small bowl using the back of a teaspoon. Bring the wine mixture to a gentle boil, then gradually drop in small pieces of the thickening paste, whisking each piece in using a wire whisk. Simmer for 1–2 minutes.

9 Scatter the mushrooms over the chicken, then pour over the wine sauce. Garnish with the chopped parsley.

Remove skin from the chicken to reduce fat

•

Replace some of the butter with oil to lower saturated fat

•

Boost flavour with herbs so that less salt is needed

Lamb tagine

With the exotic combination of meat, spices, fruits and nuts in a Moroccan tagine, fat can easily tip the balance from low to high depending on how it is cooked and the choice of meat. By choosing a lean cut of lamb and considering other ways to lighten, this recipe has more than halved the fat without losing any of its appeal.

	Classic	Lighter
Kcals	534	339
Fat	33.4 g	14.7 g
Sat fat	13.3 g	4.4 g
Salt	0.7 g	0.6 g

Per serving 339 kcals

Protein 29.9 g, carbs 22.5 g, fat 14.7 g, sat fat 4.4 g, fibre 6 g, sugar 15.3 g, salt 0.6 g

Serves 6

Prep: 35 minutes, plus overnight marinating
Cook: 2 hours 25 minutes

750 g (1 lb 10 oz) diced leg of lamb, cut into about 4cm (1½ inch) pieces), trimmed of excess fat

2 medium onions

2 teaspoons ground cumin

1½ teaspoons paprika

1 teaspoon ground cinnamon

good pinch of crushed dried chillies

good pinch of saffron threads

2 tablespoons rapeseed oil

3 garlic cloves, finely chopped

1½ teaspoons finely grated fresh root ginger

400 g (14 oz) can plum tomatoes

225 g (8 oz) can plum tomatoes

25 g (1 oz) bunch fresh coriander

140 g (5 oz) soft dried apricots, halved

400 g (14 oz) can chickpeas, drained

2 teaspoons clear honey

salt and freshly ground black pepper

1 Preheat the oven to 160°C (fan 140°C/325°F/gas mark 3). Put the meat in a large mixing bowl. Grate one of the onions, then tip it into the meat with the cumin, paprika, cinnamon, crushed chillies, saffron and 1 tablespoon of the oil. Season well with pepper and toss well together to coat. Cover and leave for 2–3 hours or preferably overnight in the fridge.

2 Chop the remaining onion. Heat the remaining oil in a large, heavy non-stick frying or sauté pan. Put in the chopped onion, garlic and ginger and fry on a medium heat for about 5 minutes, stirring often, until starting to brown. Then raise the heat slightly, add the meat and its spices and stir-fry until it's no longer pink. Stir in both cans of tomatoes. Rinse the cans out with 250 ml (9 fl oz) water and stir in. Chop half of the bunch of coriander, including the stalks, and stir it into the tagine with the apricots. Heat through and transfer to an ovenproof dish.

3 Cook in the oven for 2 hours, topping up with a bit more water if necessary to keep it all juicy. Stir in the chickpeas and honey and cook for a further 15 minutes or until the meat is really tender.

4 Separate the leaves from the remaining coriander and chop. Season the tagine with a little salt and serve scattered with the chopped coriander leaves.

Replace some of the meat with chickpeas to keep the protein up but reduce the fat, boost fibre content and count towards your five a day

Salmon teriyaki

It's a popular restaurant and takeaway dish, but salt and sugar can be high in this Japanese speciality, due to the sticky, salty-sweetness of the sauce. By adjusting some of the traditional ingredients and combining with handy store-cupboard ones, it's quick to make at home, salt is halved and sugar greatly lowered but the familiar taste remains.

	Classic	Lighter
Kcals	361	269
Fat	18.2 g	15.4 g
Sat fat	3 g	2.7 g
Sugar	11.3 g	1.6 g
Salt	2.9 g	1.5 g

Per serving 269 kcals

Protein 28.7 g, carbs 2 g, fat 15.4 g, sat fat 2.7 g, fibre 0.1 g, sugar 1.6 g, salt 1.5g

Serves 4

Prep: 10 minutes
Cook: 15 minutes

2 tablespoons dark soy sauce

3 tablespoons dry white wine

2 tablespoons apple juice from concentrate

2 teaspoons white wine vinegar

2 garlic cloves, crushed

1 teaspoon finely grated fresh root ginger

4 salmon fillets, about 140 g (5 oz) each, skinned

freshly ground black pepper

1 Make the teriyaki sauce. Put the soy sauce, wine, apple juice, vinegar, garlic and ginger in a small pan with 1 tablespoon water and a grinding of pepper. Bring to the boil, then bubble for 2–3 minutes to reduce slightly. Remove and set aside.

2 Heat the grill to high. Line a baking sheet with foil and lay the salmon fillets on it. Grill the salmon, fairly near to the grill, for about 10 minutes or until done (no need to turn it), brushing a couple of times with a little of the teriyaki sauce for the last 2 minutes to glaze.

3 Warm the rest of the sauce and pour it over the salmon to serve.

TIPS

- To check when the salmon is cooked, open up the flesh slightly in the middle with the tip of a knife, and if you like it cooked all the way through, the flakes should no longer look translucent.
- Serve with fine noodles tossed with chopped fresh coriander – and a fresh green vegetable.

Extend the sauce with apple juice, which provides natural sweetness, instead of adding sugar

Mediterranean fish stew

Packed with fish, seafood and tomatoes, this dish is a pretty healthy classic. To improve things even further, it's only taken a few tweaks to maximize its benefits and lower salt and fat.

	Classic	Lighter
Kcals	311	255
Fat	7.5 g	5.2 g
Sat fat	1.1 g	0.8 g
Salt	1.8 g	0.9 g

Per serving 255 kcals

Protein 30.8 g, carbs 12.9 g, fat 5.2 g, sat fat 0.8 g, fibre 6 g, sugar 9 g, salt 0.9 g

Serves 4

Prep: 20 minutes
Cook: 25 minutes

1 fennel bulb, about 300 g (11 oz) total weight

1 tablespoon olive oil, plus 1 teaspoon

1 small carrot, diced

2 celery sticks, diced

1 large or 2 small shallots, finely chopped

2 garlic cloves, finely chopped

175 ml (6 fl oz) dry white wine

150 ml (¼ pint) tomato juice

400 g (14 oz) can cherry tomatoes, in natural juice

good pinch of saffron threads

good pinch of smoked paprika

4 tablespoons chopped basil

250 g (9 oz) cherry tomatoes on the vine

500 g (1 lb 2oz) skinless haddock or cod fillets, cut into 4–5 cm (1½–2 inch) chunks

12 raw (or cooked), peeled king prawns, with tails left on

salt and freshly ground pepper

include fennel, carrot and celery and extra cherry tomatoes to top up the five a day, vitamin c, fibre and flavour

1 Preheat the oven to 200°C (fan 180°C/400°F/gas mark 6). Trim, then quarter the fennel lengthways and cut out and discard the central core. Finely chop the fennel. Heat the 1 tablespoon oil in a large, deep sauté or frying pan. Tip in the fennel, carrot, celery, shallot and garlic and fry for 3–4 minutes. Raise the heat, pour in the wine and simmer for a few minutes until reduced by a third. Mix the tomato juice with 150 ml (¼ pint) water. Pour into the pan with the can of tomatoes, saffron, paprika and 2 tablespoons of the basil. Season with pepper, bring to the boil, then bubble away gently for about 8 minutes to cook the vegetables and reduce the liquid very slightly.

2 While the vegetables are cooking, remove the tomatoes from the vine and cut in half widthways. Lay them on a baking sheet, scatter over 1 tablespoon of the remaining basil, season with pepper and drizzle with the 1 teaspoon oil. Roast in the oven for 8–10 minutes until the tomatoes are softened but still holding their shape.

3 Place the fish and prawns (if using raw ones) in the sauté pan with the vegetables and simmer gently for 4–5 minutes or until they are just cooked and no longer opaque. If using cooked prawns, add them for the last minute or two to heat through. Season with a pinch of salt.

4 Spoon the fish and vegetables into the middle of large, wide bowls, spoon the liquid around and serve scattered with the roasted tomatoes and sprinkled with the last of the chopped basil.

Risotto primavera

This dish is mainly rice cooked with lots of fresh green seasonal vegetables, but there are hidden extras. Butter is often used to fry the rice at the beginning, and a generous amount is usually stirred in at the end – as is Parmesan – to inject flavour and richness. I looked at what could be added instead to develop the flavour.

	Classic	Lighter
Kcals	715	475
Fat	31 g	10.4 g
Sat fat	16 g	2.8 g
Salt	2.1 g	0.3 g

Per serving 475 kcals

Protein 18.6 g, carbs 70.5 g, fat 10.4 g, sat fat 2.8 g, fibre 9.8 g, sugar 5.2 g, salt 0.3 g

Serves 4

Prep: 40 minutes
Cook: 35 minutes

2 tablespoons olive oil

350 g (12 oz) asparagus spears, trimmed and sliced into 5 cm (2 inch) diagonal lengths

9 spring onions, ends trimmed and sliced

175 g (6 oz) fresh or frozen peas

250 g (9 oz) fresh or frozen broad beans, shelled

2 tablespoons shredded basil

2 tablespoons snipped chives

1 tablespoon finely chopped mint

finely grated zest of 1 lemon

1.7 litres (3 pints) vegetable stock

4 shallots, finely chopped

3 plump garlic cloves, finely chopped

300 g (11 oz) carnaroli or arborio rice

150 ml (¼ pint) dry white wine

25 g (1 oz) Parmesan cheese or vegetarian alternative, grated

25 g (1 oz) rocket

freshly ground black pepper

1 Heat half the oil in a large, wide non-stick frying pan. Tip in the asparagus and stir-fry over a medium-high heat for about 4 minutes or until nicely browned all over. Stir in the spring onions and fry for 1–2 minutes with the asparagus until browned. Remove, season with pepper and set aside.

2 Cook the peas and beans separately in a little boiling water for 3 minutes each, then drain each through a sieve. When the broad beans are cool enough to handle, pop them out of their skins. Set the peas and beans aside.

3 Mix the basil, chives, mint and lemon zest together in a small bowl and season with pepper. Set aside.

4 Pour the stock into a saucepan and keep it on a very low heat. Pour the remaining oil into a large, wide sauté pan. Tip in the shallots and garlic and fry for 3–4 minutes until soft and only slightly brown. Stir in the rice and continue to stir for 1–2 minutes over a medium-high heat. As it starts to

sizzle, pour in the wine and stir again until the wine has been absorbed. Start to stir in the hot stock, 1½ ladlefuls at a time, so that it simmers and is absorbed after each addition. Keep stirring the whole time, to keep the risotto creamy. Continue adding the stock as above – after 20 minutes the rice should be soft with a bit of chew in the middle. If it isn't, add more stock – you should still have at least a ladleful of stock left at this point. Season with pepper; you shouldn't need to add any salt.

5 Take the pan off the heat. Pour over a ladleful of the remaining stock to keep the mixture fluid, then scatter over all the vegetables, a grinding of pepper, half of the herb mix and half of the cheese. Cover and let the risotto sit for 3–4 minutes to rest. Gently stir everything together, if necessary adding a drop more remaining stock for good consistency. Ladle into serving dishes and serve topped with a small pile of rocket and the remaining herbs and cheese scattered over.

OTHER WAYS TO USE...

The cooked rice mixture
Instead of stirring spring vegetables through at the end, scatter the rice with a mix of roasted vegetables, such as peppers, courgette, onion and squash. Or instead of a main meal, serve the finished risotto as an accompaniment to grilled chicken or poached salmon.

Replace butter with olive oil, using less of it

•

Increase the vegetables to provide three of your five-a-day

•

Reduce the amount of Parmesan to lower the fat further

•

Mix in a lemon zest and herb mix for extra flavour instead of extra salt

Beef Wellington

In classic recipes for this impressive entertaining centrepiece, there is layer upon layer of rich ingredients. For my healthier version, I wanted to maintain the extravagant look and taste while greatly reducing the calories and fat. The meat needs to be tied at equal intervals to hold it together – either do this yourself or ask your butcher to do it.

	Classic	Lighter
Kcals	699	350
Fat	41 g	16.6 g
Sat fat	19.3 g	5 g
Salt	1.7 g	0.8 g

Per serving 350 kcals

Protein 39.5 g, carbs 8.3 g, fat 16.6 g, sat fat 5 g, fibre 1.3 g, sugar 0.8 g, salt 0.8 g

Serves 6

Prep: 1 hour, plus soaking, cooling and resting
Cook: about 1 hour

For the beef

3 tablespoons rapeseed oil

1 kg (2 lb 4 oz) thick, lean fillet of beef, tied at equal intervals

good handful of dried porcini mushrooms

2 shallots, finely chopped

2 garlic cloves, finely chopped

140 g (5 oz) chestnut mushrooms, trimmed and very finely chopped

2 tablespoons finely chopped flat leaf parsley

1 tablespoon finely chopped tarragon

100 g (4 oz) mix of watercress, baby spinach and rocket or watercress or spinach leaves

6 sheets filo pastry, each approximately 38 x 30 cm (15 x 12 inches), about 125 g (4½ oz) total weight

For the gravy

1 teaspoon plain flour

5 tablespoons red wine

350 ml (12 fl oz) chicken stock

2 teaspoons Dijon mustard

salt and freshly ground black pepper

1 Preheat the oven to 220°C (fan 200°C/425°F/gas mark 7). Heat 2 teaspoons of the oil in a large, non-stick frying pan. Lay the beef in the pan and fry over a high heat for 5 minutes to seal, turning often. Transfer it to a roasting tin, season with pepper and a pinch of salt, then roast for 17–18 minutes (this roasts to medium-rare).

2 Meanwhile, put the porcini in a small heatproof bowl, cover with boiling water and leave for 20–30 minutes to soak.

3 Pour 1 tablespoon of the remaining oil into the same frying pan (don't wash it) that the meat was cooked in. Tip in the shallots, garlic and chestnut mushrooms and fry for 4–5 minutes, stirring often, over a high-ish heat so that all the liquid is first released from the mushrooms, then evaporated, and all are softened. Remove from the heat, stir in the parsley and tarragon, season with pepper and a pinch of salt and leave to cool.

4 Put the mix of leaves in a large heatproof bowl, pour over boiling water, leave for 30 seconds, then tip into a colander, rinse under cold running water and drain. Squeeze out all the moisture with your hands and pat dry with kitchen paper. Chop and set aside.

5 Drain the porcini, reserving 5 tablespoons of the soaking liquid for the gravy. Chop the porcini finely and stir it into the mushroom mix. Line a baking sheet with baking parchment.

6 When the beef is done, remove from the oven and let it sit in the tin for 10 minutes for any juices to be released. Lower the oven temperature to 200°C (fan 180°C/400°F/gas mark 6). Lift the beef from the tin (keep all the juices in the tin for the gravy) and lay it on kitchen paper. Leave until dry and cool enough to wrap in the filo.

7 Lay one of the filo sheets on the work surface with the short end facing you. Brush all over with a little of the remaining oil. Layer up and oil 4 more filo sheets in the same way. Remove the string from the cooled beef. Spread the chopped leaves down the middle of the pastry so that it is the same length and width as the fillet. Top with the mushroom mix and lightly press down. Lay the beef over this, with the top of the beef facing down. Bring the long sides of the filo over the beef to enclose it, then turn it over so that the join is underneath. Tuck both ends of the pastry under (trim first if necessary to reduce any excess) and place on the lined baking sheet so that all the joins are on the bottom. Brush with more oil.

8 Lay the last sheet of filo on the work surface in front of you, with one of the longest sides towards you, then cut across its width into 5 strips. Lay these one by one, slightly overlapping, over the wrapped beef, scrunching up an edge of each strip slightly as you go to give a bit of height. Carefully brush with the last of the oil, then bake for 30 minutes until golden. If the pastry starts to brown too quickly, loosely lay a piece of foil over the top. Remove the meat and let sit for 5–10 minutes before slicing.

9 Meanwhile, make the gravy. Heat the saved roasting juices in the roasting tin, stirring to deglaze. Stir in the flour. Gradually pour in the wine, stirring all the time to blend in the flour. Stir in the stock and reserved porcini liquid and bubble for about 8–10 minutes to reduce a little. It should have body, but be thinner like a 'jus'. Stir in the mustard and season with pepper. Transfer the beef to a platter, then slice thickly with a sharp knife and serve with a spoonful or two of the gravy.

OTHER WAYS TO USE...

The filling

The wilted leaves and mushroom mix make a great topping for chicken, salmon or other fish fillets. Lay both the leaves and mushroom mix on top of skinned chicken breasts or fish fillets, wrap in baking parchment parcels, then bake.

Replace puff pastry with filo to greatly reduce the fat

•

Eliminate butter and use rapeseed oil instead to keep saturated fat levels down

•

Use a non-stick frying pan

•

Make a light mushroom duxelles mix instead of classic pâté

•

Use herbs, garlic and porcini mushrooms to give flavour so that less salt is needed

Parmigiana

I've always thought this recipe needed generous amounts of oil to make it as delicious as it is. But by working out a lighter way to cook the aubergines, I've discovered that it's not really necessary. So combined with swopping cheeses, this dish hasn't lost its richness, but has reduced the fat by more than half.

	Classic	Lighter
Kcals	394	213
Fat	31.3 g	14.4 g
Sat fat	13.2 g	5.7 g
Salt	2.2 g	0.6 g

Per serving 213 kcals

Protein 10.8 g, carbs 10.2 g, fat 14.4 g, sat fat 5.7 g, fibre 6.9 g, sugar 9.4 g, salt 0.6 g

Serves 4

Prep: 35 minutes
Cook: 40 minutes

Lower the calories and the fat further by replacing most of the mozzarella with ricotta cheese

2 tablespoons olive oil, plus 1 teaspoon

1½ tablespoons lemon juice

3 aubergines, 750 g (1 lb 10 oz) total weight

2 garlic cloves, finely chopped

400 g (14 oz) can plum tomatoes

225 g (8 oz) can plum tomatoes

1 tablespoon tomato purée

1 tablespoon chopped basil, plus handful of leaves and extra leaves to garnish

100 g (4 oz) ricotta cheese

50 g (2 oz) mozzarella cheese

2 medium tomatoes, sliced

25 g (1 oz) Parmesan, grated

salt and freshly ground black pepper

1 Preheat the oven to 200°C (fan 180°C/400°F/gas mark 6). Brush a little of the 2 tablespoons oil on to 2–3 large, non-stick baking sheets (or bake the aubergines in batches). Mix the rest of the 2 tablespoons oil with the lemon juice. Slice the aubergines into 1 cm (½ inch) thick lengthways slices and lay them in a single layer on the oiled baking sheets. Brush with the oil and lemon mix, then season with pepper. Bake for about 25 minutes until golden and softened, turning halfway through if necessary.

2 Meanwhile, make a tomato sauce. Heat the 1 teaspoon oil in a medium saucepan. Tip in the garlic and fry for 1 minute. Stir in both cans of tomatoes, breaking them down with a wooden spoon as you stir. Mix in the tomato purée and the 1 tablespoon chopped basil. Season with pepper and a pinch of salt, then simmer for about 15 minutes to thicken slightly and make a spoonable sauce.

3 Spread a spoonful or two of the sauce (just a very thin layer) in the bottom of a shallow ovenproof dish, about 25 x 20 x 5 cm (10 x 8 x 2 inches). Layer one-third of the baked aubergines on top, in overlapping slices. Spread over one-third of the remaining sauce, dot half of the ricotta in small spoonfuls on the sauce and half of the mozzarella, tear and scatter over half of the basil leaves, then season with pepper. Repeat this layering with the aubergines, sauce, ricotta, mozzarella and basil, finishing with the last third of the aubergines followed by the last of the sauce. Lay the sliced tomatoes over the sauce, season with pepper, then scatter over the Parmesan.

4 Bake at the same oven temperature as before for about 15 minutes or until golden and bubbling. Serve scattered with extra basil leaves.

Fish pie

This fish pie is much easier to make than a regular one – there's no fiddling around with a roux sauce or mashing potatoes. My tasters loved the rich combination of creamy sauce, chunky fish and crisp topping despite the fact that I'd managed to lower the saturated fat by over three-quarters.

	Classic	Lighter
Kcals	676	413
Fat	38 g	15 g
Sat fat	19 g	4 g
Salt	1.22 g	1.42 g

Per serving 413 kcals

Protein 42 g, carbs 30 g, fat 15 g,
sat fat 4 g, fibre 2 g, sugar 7 g, salt 1.42 g

Serves 6

Prep: 30 minutes, plus cooling
Cook: about 1 hour

500 ml (18 fl oz) semi-skimmed milk

3 tablespoons cornflour

100 g (4 oz) cooked prawns in their shells

several sprigs of thyme, preferably lemon thyme

2 bay leaves

1 garlic clove, thinly sliced

750 g (1 lb 10 oz) unpeeled new potatoes, such as Charlotte, scrubbed

1 medium leek, trimmed, cleaned and thinly sliced (about 175 g/6 oz) total prepared weight

400 g (14 oz) skinless haddock fillet

350 g (12 oz) skinless salmon fillet

175 g (6 oz) skinless smoked haddock fillet

125 g (4½ oz) low-fat soft cheese with garlic and herbs

2 tablespoons finely chopped parsley

2 tablespoons olive oil

2 tablespoons snipped chives

freshly ground black pepper

1 Mix 3 tablespoons of the milk into the cornflour and set aside. Pour the rest of the milk into a saucepan. Peel the prawns, reserve the meat, then drop the shells and heads (wash them first if necessary) into the milk along with the sprigs of thyme, bay leaves, garlic and a grind of pepper. Bring to the boil, then remove from the heat and leave to infuse for 20 minutes.

2 Meanwhile, put the potatoes into a large pan of water, bring to the boil and simmer for 20 minutes until tender. Drain.

3 Steam the sliced leek for 3 minutes, then remove from the heat and set aside.

4 Strain the infused milk through a sieve into a large, shallow sauté pan. Lay the fish fillets in the milk. Bring to the boil, then lower the heat and simmer gently for 3 minutes. Remove from the heat and leave, covered, for 5 minutes. Use a slotted spoon to transfer all the fish to a dish and leave to cool slightly. Preheat the oven to 200°C (fan 180°C/400°F/gas mark 6).

5 Stir the slackened cornflour, then stir it into the hot milk in the sauté pan. Return the pan to the heat and stir until thickened. Briefly stir in the soft cheese, remove from the heat, then add the parsley and season with black pepper. Stir in any liquid that has drained from the fish. Break the fish into big pieces and place them in a 2 litre (3½ pint) ovenproof dish. Scatter over the prawns and leek, then season with pepper. Pour the sauce over and give a few gentle stirs to evenly distribute the sauce and combine everything without breaking up the fish.

6 Using a large fork, crush the potatoes by breaking them up (not mashing them) into chunky pieces. Mix in the oil, chives and a grind of black pepper. Spoon the potato crush over the fish. Place the dish on a baking sheet and bake for 25–30 minutes or until the sauce is bubbling and the potatoes golden. Alternatively, make the dish completely, refrigerate it for several hours or overnight, then bake at the same temperature as above for 45 minutes.

OTHER WAYS TO USE...

The fish and leek sauce
Gently mix it all together and serve over shell-shaped pasta.

Cut butter and cream from the sauce and add creaminess with light soft cheese. Intensify the taste by infusing the milk with flavourings

•

Instead of a buttery, cheesy mash, try a potato crush using olive oil

Chicken biryani

My challenge was to reduce the fat and salt, yet still retain the intricacies of the recipe with its gentle, fragrant spicing and rich, moist consistency. Serve with a cooling tomato and cucumber raita.

	Classic	Lighter
Kcals	674	485
Fat	30.5 g	11.7 g
Sat fat	6.5 g	1.5 g
Salt	2 g	0.6 g

Per serving 485 kcals

Protein 40.1 g, carbs 51.7 g, fat 11.7 g, sat fat 1.5 g, fibre 2.7 g, sugar 7.1 g, salt 0.6 g

Serves 5

Prep: 25 minutes, plus marinating and infusing
Cook: 1¼ hours

3 garlic cloves, finely grated

2 teaspoons finely grated fresh root ginger

¼ teaspoon ground cinnamon

1 teaspoon turmeric

5 tablespoons natural yogurt

600 g (1 lb 5 oz) boneless, skinless chicken breasts, cut into 5 cm (2 inch) pieces

2 tablespoons semi-skimmed milk

good pinch of saffron threads

4 medium onions

4 tablespoons rapeseed oil

½ teaspoon hot chilli powder

1 cinnamon stick, broken in half

5 cardamom pods, lightly bashed to split

3 cloves

1 teaspoon cumin seeds

280 g (10 oz) basmati rice

700 ml (1¼ pints) chicken stock

1 teaspoon garam masala

chopped mint and fresh coriander leaves, to garnish

salt and freshly ground black pepper

1 In a bowl, stir together the garlic, ginger, cinnamon, turmeric and yogurt with some pepper and ¼ teaspoon salt. Tip in the chicken pieces and stir to coat. Cover and marinate in the fridge for about 1 hour or longer if you have time. Warm the milk to tepid, stir in the saffron and leave to infuse.

2 Preheat the oven to 200°C (fan 180°C/400°F/gas mark 6). Slice each onion in half lengthways, reserve half and cut the other half into thin slices. Pour 1½ tablespoons of the oil on to a baking sheet, scatter over the sliced onion, toss to coat, then spread out in a thin, even layer. Roast for 40–45 minutes, stirring halfway, until golden.

3 Meanwhile, when the chicken has marinated, thinly slice the reserved onion. Heat 1 tablespoon of the remaining oil in a large sauté or frying pan. Fry the onion for 4–5 minutes until golden. Stir in the chicken, a spoonful at a time, frying until it is no longer opaque, before adding the next spoonful (this helps to prevent the yogurt from curdling). Once the last of the chicken has been added, stir-fry for a further 5 minutes. Stir in the chilli powder, then pour in 100 ml (3½ fl oz) water, stir well, cover and simmer on a low heat for 15 minutes. Remove and set aside.

4 Heat another 1 tablespoon of the oil in a large sauté pan, then add the cinnamon stick, cardamoms, cloves and cumin seeds. Fry briefly until their aroma is released. Add the rice and fry for 1 minute, stirring constantly. Stir in the stock and bring to the boil. Lower the heat and simmer, covered, for about 8 minutes or until all the stock has been absorbed. Remove from the heat and leave with the lid on for a few minutes so that the rice can fluff up. Stir the garam masala into the remaining oil and set aside. When the onions are roasted, remove and reduce the oven temperature to 180°C (fan 160°C/350°F/gas mark 4).

5 Spoon half of the chicken and its juices into an ovenproof dish, about 25 x 18 x 6 cm (10 x 7 x 2½ inches), then scatter over a third of the roasted onions. Remove the whole spices from the rice, then layer half of the rice over the chicken and onions. Drizzle over the spiced oil. Spoon over the rest of the chicken and a third more onions. Top with the remaining rice and drizzle over the saffron-infused milk. Scatter over the rest of the onions, cover tightly with foil and heat through in the oven for about 25 minutes. Serve scattered with the mint and coriander.

use rapeseed oil instead of butter or ghee to cut saturated fat

•

choose skinless chicken breasts to reduce the fat

•

use a good balance of spices and herbs to reduce salt

•

Roast onions instead of frying them so that they need less oil

Paella

This Spanish speciality is a harmonious mix of meat and seafood. The choice of ingredients, however, can all impact on the fat or salt content. I've tweaked things to create a recipe that still delivers an authentic taste.

	Classic	Lighter
Kcals	729	609
Fat	25 g	8.6 g
Sat fat	7.5 g	2 g
Salt	2.3 g	1.9 g

Per serving 609 kcals

Protein 48.5 g, carbs 77.5 g, fat 8.6 g, sat fat 2g, fibre 6.9 g, sugar 8.5 g, salt 1.9g

Serves 4

Prep: 25 minutes, plus infusing
Cook: 30 minutes

large pinch of saffron threads, about ¼ teaspoon

200 g (7 oz) cooked prawns, in their shells, thawed if frozen

1½ tablespoons olive oil

3 slices prosciutto, trimmed of excess fat, roughly chopped

1 onion, finely chopped

3 plump garlic cloves, finely chopped

450 g (1 lb) boneless, skinless chicken breasts, cut into cubes

1 large red pepper, cored, deseeded and chopped

1½ teaspoons paprika

½ teaspoon smoked paprika

350 g (12 oz) Spanish paella rice

600 ml (1 pint) hot chicken stock, from a good-quality cube

150 ml (¼ pint) dry white wine

200 g (7 oz) tomatoes, roughly chopped

100 g (4 oz) frozen peas

100 g (4 oz) fine green beans, stem ends trimmed and sliced into 2.5cm/ 1-inch pieces

handful of chopped flat leaf parsley

salt and freshly ground black pepper

lemon wedges, to serve

Swop chorizo for prosciutto to help lower the fat – and regain any loss of flavour by mixing in smoked paprika powder

1 Stir the saffron into 1 tablespoon hot water and set aside for the flavours to infuse while you prepare the paella. Peel the prawns, leaving the tails on.

2 Heat 1 tablespoon of the oil in a paella pan or large, deep sauté pan. Tip in the prosciutto and fry for about 1 minute or until crisp. Remove with a slotted spoon, letting any fat drain back into the pan, and set aside. Stir the onion and garlic into the pan and fry for 4–5 minutes, stirring occasionally. Pour in the remaining ½ tablespoon oil, add the chicken and stir-fry over a medium-high heat for 5 minutes. Stir in the red pepper and both paprikas, then the rice. The bottom of the pan should have lots of brown crispy bits on it, which will add flavour.

3 Pour in the stock, wine, 150ml (¼ pint) boiling water and the saffron and its liquid, scraping up the brown bits from the bottom of the pan. Tip in the chopped tomatoes, cover and cook on a medium heat for 10 minutes, stirring just occasionally. Scatter the peas and prawns on top, cover again and cook for a further 4–5 minutes or until the rice is just cooked and most of the liquid has been absorbed. Meanwhile, steam the beans for 4–5 minutes, then tip them into the pan.

4 Remove from the heat, keep the pan covered and let the paella stand for 5 minutes. Season to taste with pepper and a little salt, lightly mix, scatter over the parsley and crisp prosciutto and serve with lemon wedges.

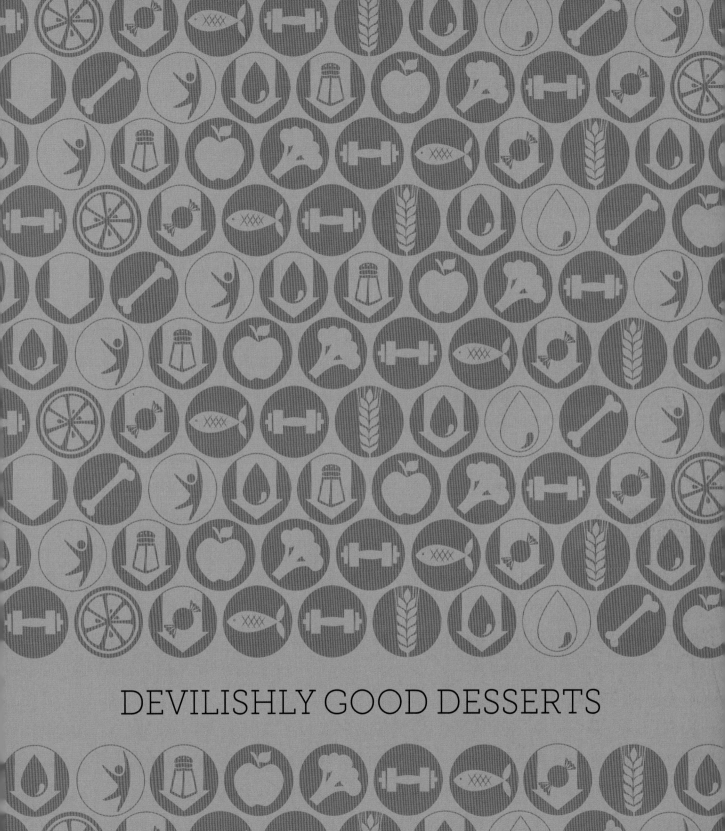

DEVILISHLY GOOD DESSERTS

New York cheesecake

A good recipe for this New York classic will capture the necessary qualities of a creamy texture, slight tangy taste and the essential seductive ooze in the centre – the sort of dessert you can't wait to dig your fork into. This one is much lighter but just as decadent.

	Classic	Lighter
Kcals	665	315
Fat	49 g	15 g
Sat fat	30.2 g	8 g
Sugar	32.6 g	28 g

Per slice 315 kcals

Protein 9 g, carbs 37 g, fat 15 g, sat fat 8 g, fibre 1 g, sugar 28 g, salt 0.89 g

Cuts into 10 slices

Prep: 25 minutes, plus cooling and chilling
Cook: 50 minutes

For the base

35 g (1¼ oz) butter

85 g (3 oz) reduced-fat digestive biscuits, finely crushed

For the filling

600 g (1 lb 5 oz) light soft cheese, at room temperature

175 g (6 oz) golden caster sugar

3 tablespoons cornflour

1½ teaspoons finely grated lemon zest

1 teaspoon lemon juice

1 teaspoon vanilla extract

3 large eggs, at room temperature, beaten

150 g (5¼ oz) fromage frais

For the topping

25 g (1 oz) golden caster sugar

225 g (8 oz) blueberries

½ teaspoon finely grated lime zest

100 g (4 oz) fromage frais

1 Preheat the oven to 180°C (fan 160°C/350°F/gas mark 4). Line a 20 cm (8 inch) loose-bottomed or springform cake tin with baking parchment and stand it on a baking sheet. Melt the butter in the saucepan and stir in the biscuit crumbs. Press the mix into the base of the tin, then bake for 10 minutes. Remove from the oven and increase the oven temperature to 240°C (fan 220°C/475°F/gas mark 9).

2 For the filling, beat the soft cheese just until smooth with an electric hand mixer on low speed. Gradually add the sugar, also on a low speed, then the cornflour without overbeating. Scrape the sides of the bowl. Slowly whisk in the lemon zest and juice, the vanilla, then the eggs. Scrape the sides of the bowl, then finally whisk in the fromage frais. The mixture should be smooth and quite runny.

3 Pour the filling over the crumb base. Jiggle the tin to level the mix and squash any surface bubbles with a teaspoon. Bake for 10 minutes, then lower the heat to 110°C (fan 90°C/225°F/gas mark ¼). Bake for another 25 minutes and, if you are using an electric oven, leave the oven door slightly ajar for the first 3 minutes. After the 25 minutes, shake the tin and there should be a wobble in the centre of the filling. If left until firmer, it is more likely to crack later. Turn off the oven, keep the door closed and leave the cake in for 2 hours. Open the door, loosen the top edges of the cake with a round-bladed knife, then leave in the oven to cool gently for another 1–1½ hours.

4 Meanwhile, put the sugar for the topping in a small pan with 3 tablespoons water. Bring to a simmer, stirring to dissolve the sugar, then let it bubble for 1–2 minutes to make a thin syrup. Tip in the blueberries, gently stir and cook for about 1 minute, just to slightly burst the fruit and release the purple juices. Stir in the lime zest, then leave to cool.

5 Spread the fromage frais over the top of the cooled cheesecake. Cover with foil and chill for at least 4 hours (or overnight). Remove from the fridge 1 hour before serving, loosen the sides of the cheesecake completely, remove from the tin, then slide on to a plate, peeling off the paper as you do so. Slice with a sharp knife and serve each wedge topped with a spoonful of the syrupy blueberries.

Reduce fat by making the crust thinner and using reduced-fat biscuits

•

Use light soft cheese instead of full-fat and fromage frais instead of soured cream

•

Use whole eggs rather than whole eggs plus extra yolks

•

Omit sugar from the base and reduce it in the filling

Coffee panna cotta

This is one of those desserts that is hard to resist. However, as it is traditionally made with cream and very little else, fat levels shoot right up. This version won't disappoint – it's creamy with a silky smooth texture but has far less fat and fewer calories.

	Classic	Lighter
Kcals	591	270
Fat	54.2 g	19.2 g
Sat fat	33.7 g	12.2 g
Sugar	23.4 g	17.7 g

Per serving 270 kcals

Protein 6.4 g, carbs 17.8 g, fat 19.2 g, sat fat 12.2 g, fibre 0g, sugar 17.7 g, salt 0.2 g

Serves 4

Prep: 15 minutes, plus infusing, cooling and several hours chilling (or overnight chilling)
Cook: 3 minutes

125 ml (4 fl oz) whipping cream

50 g (2 oz) golden caster sugar

½ vanilla pod, slit lengthways

2 small gelatine leaves, each 12 x 6 cm (4½ x 2½ inches)

2 teaspoons instant coffee granules

250 g (9 oz) Greek yogurt

150 ml (¼ pint) buttermilk

sifted cocoa powder, for dusting

1 Put the cream and sugar in a small saucepan. Scrape in the seeds from the vanilla pod, then drop in the pod. Stir over a low heat until the sugar has dissolved. Bring the mixture just to the boil, then remove from the heat and leave to infuse for 5 minutes.

2 Meanwhile, lay the gelatine leaves in a shallow dish and pour over enough cold water to cover them. Leave to soak for 4–5 minutes.

3 Remove the gelatine leaves from the water, squeeze well to remove the excess water, then stir the leaves into the hot cream until dissolved. Stir in the coffee granules until they are also dissolved. Leave the mixture to become cold, stirring occasionally. Keep checking so that you can catch it before it starts to set. You want it to stay runny.

4 Discard the vanilla pod. Beat the yogurt and buttermilk together in a large bowl, then gradually pour and beat in the cold coffee mixture. Transfer it to a jug and pour into 4 small (150 ml/¼ pint) dariole moulds. Chill for 4–5 hours or overnight.

5 To loosen when ready to serve, dip each mould into a bowl of very hot water (to just below the rim) for a few seconds only. Turn each one out on to a small plate or saucer. Re-dip if they don't fall out the first time. Lightly dust with cocoa.

Replace double cream with whipping cream, Greek yogurt and buttermilk, to greatly reduce fat and calories

Chocolate tart

A chocolate tart with a rich taste – but with two-thirds less fat than the classic. For a little extra, you can serve each slice with 1 tablespoon half-fat crème fraîche. The fat will increase to 15.3 g (sat fat 8.6 g) per serving.

	Classic	Lighter
Kcals	542	243
Fat	39.4 g	13.4 g
Sat fat	24.2 g	7.3 g
Sugar	25.1 g	13.7 g

Per slice 243 kcals

Protein 4.4 g, carbs 25.8 g, fat 13.4 g, sat fat 7.3 g, fibre 1.3 g, sugar 13.7 g, salt 0.3 g

Cuts into 8 slices

Prep: 35 minutes, plus chilling and cooling
Cook: 25 minutes

For the pastry

140 g (5 oz) plain flour, plus extra for dusting

50 g (2 oz) butter, cut into pieces

2 teaspoons cocoa powder

1 tablespoon icing sugar

1 tablespoon rapeseed oil

1 medium egg yolk

For the filling

100 g (4 oz) dark chocolate, 70% cocoa solids, very finely chopped

1 tablespoon cocoa powder, plus an extra ½ teaspoon for dusting

¾ teaspoon instant coffee granules

½ teaspoon vanilla extract

2 tablespoons semi-skimmed milk

2 medium egg whites

2 tablespoons dark muscovado sugar

85 g (3 oz) half-fat crème fraîche, plus extra to serve (optional)

1 Tip the flour into a mixing bowl and remove 2 teaspoons (the cocoa will replace it later). Add the butter and rub into the flour with your fingertips until the mixture resembles fine breadcrumbs. Sift in the cocoa and icing sugar, then, using a round-bladed knife, stir in the oil, egg yolk and 1½–2 tablespoons cold water until the dough comes together. Gently gather into a ball, then roll out on a lightly floured surface until large enough to fit a 20 cm (8 inch) round, 3.5 cm (1½ inch) deep, loose-bottomed flan tin. Ease the pastry into the tin, leaving a slight overhang. Lightly prick the base with a fork, then chill for about 10 minutes.

2 Preheat the oven to 190°C (fan 170°C/375°F/gas mark 5). Place the tin on a baking sheet. Line the pastry with foil and fill with baking beans. Bake blind for 15 minutes or until set. Carefully lift out the beans and paper, then bake the pastry case for another 10 minutes or until the base is cooked. Remove, carefully trim off the overhanging pastry with a sharp knife, to give the pastry a flat edge, then leave until completely cold.

3 To make the filling, put the chocolate in a large heatproof bowl that will fit over a pan of simmering water without touching it. Mix the cocoa, coffee and vanilla with the milk. Pour over the chocolate. Sit the bowl over a pan of gently simmering water, stir, then immediately remove the pan from the heat, with the bowl of chocolate still over the water, stirring occasionally to check when melted. Stir the melted chocolate – it will be quite thick. Stir in 2 tablespoons boiling water and the chocolate will immediately thin down and become silky smooth. Take the bowl off the pan and leave to cool slightly.

4 Whisk the egg whites to stiff peaks, then whisk in the sugar until thick and glossy. Fold the crème fraîche into the cooled chocolate. Fold one-third of the egg whites into the chocolate mixture using a large metal spoon, then very gently fold in the remaining whites, a third at a time, until evenly mixed in. Remove the pastry case from the tin and place on a serving plate. Spoon the filling into the case, then spread out gently and evenly. Chill for about 3 hours, or overnight, before serving. Serve with a dusting of cocoa and half-fat crème fraîche, if you like.

Replace some of the butter in the pastry with rapeseed oil to reduce saturated fat

•

Instead of cream, use less half-fat crème fraîche and maintain bulk and texture with whisked egg white

•

Choose a good-quality dark chocolate so that you can use less and keep fat lower. Strengthen the rich taste with a little cocoa powder

Strawberry fool

Crush some ripe strawberries, fold them into a bowlful of sweetened whipped double cream and you have a winning flavour combination for a fruit fool. Strawberries and cream are great partners, but cream makes this a very high-fat dessert. By switching ingredients around, I've found other ways to create the desired richness and reduce fat dramatically.

	Classic	Lighter
Kcals	452	169
Fat	40.4 g	9.1 g
Sat fat	25 g	5.8 g
Sugar	20 g	15 g

Per serving 169 kcals

Protein 5.3 g, carbs 15 g, fat 9.1 g, sat fat 5.8 g, fibre 1.8 g, sugar 15 g, salt 0.1 g

Serves 4

Prep: 20 minutes, plus chilling

500 g (1 lb 2 oz) fresh strawberries, hulled

1 tablespoon plus 1 teaspoon golden caster sugar

2 teaspoons crème de cassis

50 ml (2 fl oz) whipping cream

140 g (5 oz) Greek yogurt

85 g (3 oz) half-fat crème fraîche

1 Roughly chop then roughly mash the strawberries together with the sugar and cassis using a fork if the strawberries are ripe enough, or briefly in a few short bursts using a food processor or stick hand blender. Try not to over-process as it's good to leave a few chunky pieces of fruit.

2 Tip the strawberries into a fine sieve set over a bowl and leave for about 10 minutes for the excess juice to drain into it. This makes sure the fool is not too liquidy.

3 Whisk the whipping cream in a large bowl to soft peaks, then fold in the yogurt and crème fraîche. Fold in the crushed strawberries and reserve the drained juice. Spoon the strawberry fool into glasses or small bowls and chill for 1–2 hours before serving. Serve with the drained juice.

use Greek yogurt, half-fat crème fraîche and a little whipping cream to replace double cream and lower the fat and saturated fat

Fruity sponge pudding and custard

One way I found to make this sponge recipe light yet comforting was to layer in more fruit. To simplify the cooking I switched from steaming the pudding traditionally on the hob to 'steaming' it in the oven, in a roasting tin with water added.

	Classic	Lighter
Kcals	529	318
Fat	28 g	14 g
Sat fat	16 g	8 g
Sugar	50 g	27 g

Per serving (pudding) 318 kcals

Protein 5 g, carbs 45 g, fat 14 g, sat fat 8 g, sugar 27 g, salt 0.69 g

	Classic	Lighter
Kcals	209	115
Fat	14.3 g	7 g
Sat fat	7.2 g	4 g
Sugar	17.5 g	8 g

Per serving (custard) 115 kcals

Protein 3 g, carbs 11 g, fat 7 g, sat fat 4 g, sugar 8 g, salt 0.10 g

Serves 6

Prep: 20 minutes
Cook: 1¼ hours

For the pudding

1 large eating apple, peeled, cored and quartered

140 g (5 oz) fresh or frozen blackberries or raspberries

50 g (2 oz) golden caster sugar, plus 2 tablespoons

140 g (5 oz) plain flour

1½ teaspoons baking powder

50 g (2 oz) light muscovado sugar

85 g (3 oz) butter, at room temperature, plus extra for greasing

2 large eggs

2 tablespoons semi-skimmed milk

finely grated zest of 1 orange

For the custard

25 g (1 oz) golden caster sugar

1½ teaspoons custard powder

1½ teaspoons cornflour

300 ml (½ pint) semi-skimmed milk

1 large egg yolk

1 vanilla pod

200 ml (7 fl oz) half-fat crème fraîche

1 Very lightly butter a 1 litre (1¾ pint) pudding basin. Preheat the oven to 180°C (fan 160°C/350°F/gas mark 4). Coarsely grate one of the apple quarters and thinly slice the rest. Combine the sliced apple and berries, toss with the 2 tablespoons caster sugar and spoon half into the bottom of the basin.

2 Mix together the flour and baking powder. Beat both the sugars and butter together in a large bowl with an electric hand mixer until light and creamy. Break in 1 egg and beat well, then beat in the second egg (the mixture will look curdled). Sift half of the flour mixture over the sponge mixture and fold in gently. Carefully stir in half of the milk, then repeat with the rest of the flour and milk, followed by the orange zest and reserved grated apple.

3 Spoon two-thirds of the sponge mixture over the fruit mix in the basin and level off. Spread the rest of the fruit on top, followed by the remaining sponge mixture. Place the basin in a small roasting tin half-filled with hot water. Bake for 1¼ hours (lay foil over the top for the last 15 minutes if it is browning too quickly) or until a skewer inserted in the middle comes out clean.

4 While the pudding is baking, make the custard. In a mixing bowl, mix the sugar, custard powder and cornflour with 1 tablespoon of the milk to make a paste. Beat in the egg yolk. Pour the remaining milk into a pan, slit the vanilla pod lengthways and scrape in the vanilla seeds. Add the pod to the milk and bring just to the boil. Pour the milk over the cornflour paste, stir, then pour into a clean pan. Cook over a medium heat, stirring all the time, until it is thick enough to coat the back of a spoon. Remove from the heat and stir in the crème fraîche.

5 Loosen the pudding from the sides of the basin with a round-bladed knife and carefully invert it on to a serving plate. Serve with the custard.

Use less butter and fewer eggs in the pudding and add semi-skimmed milk to reduce the fat

•

Replace full-fat milk with semi-skimmed in the custard, replace some egg yolks with custard powder and cornflour and replace cream with half-fat crème fraîche to reduce the fat further

•

Replace some of the sugar in the pudding with orange zest and fresh fruit for flavour

Treacle sponge

Much fat and sugar is used in the classic version, but with some changes and reductions I've kept the pudding light and moist with just the right balance of sweetness.

	Classic	Lighter
Kcals	540	359
Fat	27.8 g	12.6 g
Sat fat	16.5 g	3.7 g
Sugar	46.9 g	33.1 g

Per pudding 359 kcals

Protein 7.4 g, carbs 53.6 g, fat 12.6 g, sat fat 3.7 g, fibre 1.2 g, sugar 33.1 g, salt 0.9 g

Makes 6

Prep: 25 minutes
Cook: 20–25 minutes

5 tablespoons golden syrup

1 small orange (½ teaspoon finely grated zest and 2 tablespoons, plus 1 teaspoon juice)

175 g (6 oz) self-raising flour

1½ teaspoons baking powder

100 g (4 oz) light muscovado sugar

25 g (1 oz) ground almonds

2 large eggs

175 g (6 oz) natural yogurt

1 teaspoon black treacle

25 g (1 oz) butter, melted

2 tablespoons rapeseed oil, plus ¼ teaspoon for greasing

1 Preheat the oven to 180°C (fan 160°C/350°F/gas mark 4). Grease 6 x 200 ml (7 fl oz) pudding tins with ¼ teaspoon rapeseed oil, then sit them on a baking sheet. Stir together 4 tablespoons of the golden syrup, the orange zest and the 2 tablespoons orange juice and spoon a little into the bottom of each tin.

2 Place the flour, baking powder, sugar and ground almonds in a large mixing bowl and make a well in the centre. Beat the eggs in a separate bowl, then stir in the yogurt and treacle. Pour this mixture, along with the melted butter and 2 tablespoons oil, into the dry mixture and stir together briefly with a large metal spoon, just so that everything is well combined. Divide the mixture evenly between the tins. Bake for 20–25 minutes or until the puddings have risen to the top of the tins and feel firm.

3 Mix together the remaining 1 tablespoon golden syrup and 1 teaspoon orange juice to drizzle over as a sauce. To serve, if the pudding tops have peaked slightly, slice off to level so that they sit upright when turned out. Loosen around the sides with a round-bladed knife, then turn out on to plates. Scrape out any syrupy bits remaining in the tins and put on top of the puddings, then drizzle a little of the syrup sauce over and around each one.

use yogurt and rapeseed oil instead of all butter in the pudding mixture to reduce the fat and saturated fat

Tiramisu

This recipe has been one of the the most requested when it comes to tackling a traditional recipe to make lighter. Everyone is concerned about the fat, but there is a lovely creamy taste that needs to stay, so this was about balancing a combination of cheeses and crème fraîche.

	Classic	Lighter
Kcals	442	220
Fat	30.6 g	10.1 g
Sat fat	17.7 g	5.8 g
Sugar	24.9 g	17.4 g

Per serving 220 kcals

Protein 5.7 g, carbs 25.5 g, fat 10.1 g, sat fat 5.8 g, fibre 0.3 g, sugar 17.4 g, salt 0.25 g

Serves 8

Prep: 35 minutes, plus cooling and chilling
Cook: 10 minutes

For the sponge layer

250 ml (9 fl oz) strong hot coffee, preferably made using freshly ground coffee

1 tablespoon golden caster sugar

4 tablespoons Marsala

18 sponge fingers (boudoir biscuits)

For the filling

1 tablespoon golden caster sugar

1 tablespoon cornflour

150 ml (¼ pint) semi-skimmed milk

1 medium egg

½ vanilla pod, slit lengthways

85 g (3 oz) half-fat crème fraîche

1 tablespoon Marsala

140 g (5 oz) light mascarpone cheese

100 g (4 oz) light soft cheese

½ teaspoon sifted cocoa powder, for dusting

fresh raspberries, to decorate (optional)

1 First make the coffee soaking liquid for the sponge fingers. Stir the coffee and sugar together, then pour into a shallow heatproof dish. Stir in the Marsala and leave to cool.

2 Meanwhile, prepare the filling. Put the sugar and cornflour into a medium saucepan, preferably non-stick. Stir in 1 tablespoon of the milk to make a thin, smooth paste. Separate the egg, putting the white into a mixing bowl and setting it aside, and dropping the yolk into the saucepan. Beat the yolk into the cornflour paste, then stir in the rest of the milk. Scrape the seeds from the vanilla pod into the pan, then drop in the pod. Cook over a medium-low heat for about 8–10 minutes without letting the mixture boil, stirring all the time, until the mixture thickly coats the back of a wooden spoon. Remove from the heat, then stir in the crème fraîche and the Marsala. Transfer the mixture to a bowl, cover the surface with clingfilm and leave until cold.

3 To assemble, line a 23 x 13 x 6 cm (9 x 5 x 2½ inch) loaf tin with clingfilm, leaving an overhang at the top. Beat together the mascarpone and soft cheese, then stir into the rest of the cold filling. Whisk the egg white to stiff peaks and gently fold into the filling using a large metal spoon.

4 Dip one of the sponge fingers in the coffee mixture, rolling it around briefly, for a few seconds only, to coat and soak in, then lift it out before it has a chance to get too soggy. If left in the coffee, it will disintegrate. Lay it lengthways in the bottom of the tin. Do the same with 5 more of the sponge fingers, trimming to fit if necessary so that they cover the bottom of the tin. Remove the vanilla pod from the filling. Spoon over half of the filling, spreading it to cover the biscuits, then repeat the biscuit dipping with 6 more of the sponge fingers. Spoon and spread over the rest of the filling, then dip and lay the rest of the sponge fingers over the top. Bring the clingfilm overhang over to cover. Chill overnight.

5 To serve, invert on to a serving plate and carefully peel off the clingfilm. Dust the top with the cocoa and scatter with raspberries, if you like. Slice and serve on the same day.

Reduce egg yolks and sugar by making a low-fat custard instead of a sabayon

•

Swap full-fat mascarpone for a mix of light mascarpone and light soft cheese

•

Cut down the amount of mascarpone and extend the filling instead with a whisked egg white

•

Serve smaller portions by making the dessert in a loaf tin, then serving in slices

Lemon tart

This tangy, creamy-rich dessert is particularly hard to alter. However, I've found ways to lower both fat and sugar, yet retain the sweet butteriness of the pastry and the seductive taste of the filling.

	Classic	Lighter
Kcals	323	186
Fat	18 g	9 g
Sat fat	9 g	4 g
Sugar	27 g	15 g

Per serving 186 kcals

protein 4 g, carbs 24 g, fat 9 g, sat fat 4 g, fibre 0 g, sugar 15 g, salt 0.14 g

Cuts into 12 slender slices

Prep: 35 minutes plus chilling
  and standing
Cook: 50–55 minutes

For the pastry

50 g (2 oz) butter, cut into pieces

140 g (5 oz) plain flour, plus extra for dusting

1 tablespoon sifted icing sugar

1 tablespoon extra virgin rapeseed oil

1 medium egg yolk

For the filling

3 medium eggs, plus 2 medium egg whites

140 g (5 oz) icing sugar, plus extra for dusting

2 tablespoooons finely grated lemon zest

125 ml (4 fl oz) lemon juice

200 ml (7 fl oz) half-fat crème fraîche

1   In a mixing bowl, rub the butter into the flour with your fingertips until the mixture resembles like fine breadcrumbs. Stir in the icing sugar, then make a well and use a round-bladed knife to stir in the oil, egg yolk and 1½–2 tablespoons cold water until the dough comes together. Without overhandling, gather into a ball. On a lightly floured surface, roll out to fit a 23 x 2 cm (9 x ¾ inch) deep loose-bottomed flan tin. Ease the pastry into the tin, then trim the edges by rolling the rolling pin over the top. Press the pastry into the flutes so that it sits very slightly proud of the edge. Lightly prick the pastry base with a fork, then chill for about 10 minutes. Preheat the oven to 190°C (fan 170°C/375°F/gas mark 5).

2   Beat the eggs and egg whites together in a mixing bowl with a wooden spoon until well mixed. Sift the icing sugar into a separate bowl, then gradually beat in the eggs. If the mix is at all lumpy, simply beat with a wire whisk. Stir in the lemon zest and juice. Leave to stand while you bake the pastry case so that the lemon flavour can develop.

3   Sit the chilled pastry case on a baking sheet. Line with baking parchment and baking beans and bake blind for 20 minutes until well set. Carefully lift out the beans and paper, then bake the pastry case for another 3–5 minutes until the base is cooked and pale golden.

4   Strain the lemon mixture through a sieve. Beat the crème fraîche in a mixing bowl until smooth, then slowly stir in the lemon mix until well blended. Transfer to a jug, then carefully pour two-thirds into the warm pastry case. Place in the oven with the oven shelf half out, pour in the rest of the filling, then carefully slide the shelf back in. Reduce the heat to 150°C (fan 130°C/300°F/gas mark 2). Bake for 25–30 minutes until set with a slight wobble in the middle. Cool for about an hour, then serve with a light dusting of icing sugar. Best eaten the same day.

Reduce fat by replacing some of the butter in the pastry with rapeseed oil. Cut down on egg yolks in the filling. Replace cream with half-fat crème fraîche

Blueberry trifle

In search of the lightest, most voluptuous trifle, I carefully considered each layer to maintain the recipe's elegance. The custard, cake and fruit layers can be made a day ahead ready for assembling.

	Classic	Lighter
Kcals	713 g	292
Fat	53 g	18 g
Sat fat	28 g	10 g
Sugar	34 g	20 g

Per serving 292 kcals

Protein 8g, carbs 26g, fat 18g, sat fat 10g, fibre 1g, sugar 20g, salt 0.28g

Serves 8

Prep: 30 minutes plus cooling
  and chilling
Cook: 30 minutes

For the custard

25 g (1 oz) golden caster sugar

2 teaspoons custard powder

2½ teaspoons cornflour

350 ml (12 fl oz) semi-skimmed milk

1 large egg yolk

1 vanilla pod, slit lengthways

200 ml (7 fl oz) half-fat crème fraîche

For the cake

rapeseed oil, for greasing

50 g (2 oz) golden caster sugar

2 large eggs

50 g (2 oz) self-raising flour

2 tablespoons wild blueberry 'no added sugar' fruit spread

3 tablespoons Marsala

For the fruit

2 tablespoons golden caster sugar

finely grated zest of 1 small lime

225 g (8 oz) fresh blueberries

For the topping

200 g (8 oz) Greek yogurt

250 g (9 oz) light mascarpone

2 teaspoons golden caster sugar

1 First make the custard. In a mixing bowl, blend the sugar, custard powder and cornflour with 1 tablespoon of the milk to make a runny paste, then beat in the egg yolk. Pour the remaining milk into a pan, scrape in the vanilla seeds and add the pod, then allow to come just to the boil. Stir the hot milk into the cornflour paste, then pour into a clean pan. Cook over a medium heat, stirring all the time, until thickened. Remove from the heat, then stir in the crème fraîche until smooth. Pour the custard into a bowl, cover the surface with cling film to stop a skin forming and allow to cool, then chill until completely cold.

2 Make the cake: preheat the oven to 180°C (fan 160°C/350°F/gas mark 4). Lightly grease a 20 cm (8 inch) round cake tin with rapeseed oil, then line the base with baking parchment. Put the sugar and eggs into a bowl. Whisk with an electric hand mixer for 5 minutes until the mixture is very thick, paler in colour and the consistency of whipped cream. Sift over the flour and quickly, but lightly, fold it in. Spoon the mixture into the tin and carefully level it, being careful not to squash it. Bake for 25 minutes until risen, then remove and cool on a wire rack. Peel off the lining paper. Halve the cake so that you have a semi-circle. (The other half can be frozen for another time.) Split the semi-circle in half with a knife, then sandwich back together with the fruit spread.

3 Put the sugar and lime zest for the fruit into a pan with 2 tablespoons water. Bring slowly to the boil until the sugar has dissolved, then bubble for 1½–2 minutes until syrupy. Tip in the blueberries, then cook very briefly, stirring once or twice only, just until they start to burst and release their juices (but still stay whole) and you get a purple syrup. Set aside to cool.

4 The sponge and custard layers can be built up to 2–3 hours ahead of when you want to serve the trifle. Cut the jammy sponge into cubes, then place in the base of a glass dish. Drizzle over the Marsala. Keep about one-quarter of the berries back for the top, then spoon the rest over the sponge with a little syrup. Discard the pod from the custard, then pour the custard over the fruit.

5 Just before you are ready to serve the trifle, beat the yogurt, mascarpone and sugar together until smooth and creamy. Pile the mixture on to the custard, then drizzle over the reserved fruit and syrup. Use a skewer to swirl some of the juices through the creamy topping. Serve straight away, or the syrup will discolour the topping. This is best eaten the same day.

Make a fat-free sponge for the base

•

Reduce the egg yolks in the custard and replace cream with half-fat crème fraîche. Use light mascarpone and Greek yogurt for the topping instead of cream

Apple tart

A rich, sweet and fruity tart in buttery pastry is the perfect way to end a meal. Lowering the fat and sugar that can be hidden between its layers makes this version less of a guilty treat, but the taste satisfaction remains high.

	Classic	Lighter
Kcals	376	260
Fat	19.9 g	11.3 g
Sat fat	13.6 g	5.8 g
Sugar	24.8 g	19.8 g

Per serving 260 kcals

Protein 2.7 g, carbs 31.4 g, fat 11.3 g, sat fat 5.8 g, fibre 4.4 g, sugar 19.8 g, salt 0.4g

Serves 6

Prep: 35 minutes, plus cooling
Cook: 50 minutes

For the purée

400 g (14 oz) eating apples, such as Cox's, peeled, cored and roughly chopped

3 tablespoons apple juice

½ teaspoon vanilla extract

For the pastry and topping

250 g (9 oz) bought puff pastry

plain flour, for dusting

550 g (1 l b 4 oz) eating apples, such as Cox's (about 4), peeled, cored and thinly sliced

3 teaspoons icing sugar

1 tablespoon apricot conserve

1 Put the apples for the purée in a medium saucepan, pour in the apple juice and simmer, covered, for 20–25 minutes or until really tender, keeping the heat low so that they don't dry out. Remove from the heat, mash with a fork to a rough purée, stir in the vanilla extract and leave to cool.

2 Preheat the oven to 220°C (fan 200°C/425°F/gas mark 7). On a lightly floured surface, roll the pastry out to a very thin circle, about 33 cm (13 inches) in diameter. Roll the edge over to make a narrow rim, so that you have a circle about 30 cm (12 inches) in diameter. Spread the cooled apple purée over the base, right up to the rim. Starting from the outside edge and going right up to the rim, arrange the sliced apples for the topping in neat, concentric circles over the purée. Sift over 2 teaspoons of the icing sugar.

3 Bake for about 20 minutes or until the apples are soft. Sift the rest of the icing sugar over and return to the oven for 5 more minutes so that the apples can start to get tinged brown at the edges.

4 Mix the apricot conserve with 1 tablespoon warm water, then brush it over the baked apple slices and pastry edges to glaze.

Cut down on sugar by using eating apples – instead of cooking ones – for their natural sweetness

Vanilla ice cream

Good ice cream, by its very nature, is high in fat and sugar. So this recipe required some chemistry wizardry, as sugar stops ice cream from being an ice cube and you need a certain amount of fat for taste and texture.

	Classic	Lighter
Kcals	285	148
Fat	23 g	8 g
Sat fat	12 g	4 g
Sugar	16.6 g	15 g

Per serving 148 kcals

Protein 4 g, carbs 17 g, fat 8 g, sat fat 4 g, fibre 0 g, sugar 15 g, salt 0.11 g

Makes 8 scoops

Prep: 10 minutes, plus cooling, churning or stirring and freezing
Cook: 10 minutes

85 g (3 oz) golden granulated or caster sugar

1½ teaspoons custard powder

1½ teaspoons cornflour

500 ml (18 fl oz) full-fat milk

2 large egg yolks

1 vanilla pod, slit lengthways

200 ml (7 fl oz) half-fat crème fraîche

lightly crushed fresh raspberries, to serve

1 Freeze the canister from the ice-cream machine in advance if your machine requires you to do so. You can also make this recipe without using a machine.

2 In a mixing bowl, mix the sugar, custard powder and cornflour with 2 tablespoons of the milk to make a thin paste. Beat in the egg yolks. Pour the rest of the milk into a pan, scrape in the vanilla seeds and add the pod, then bring to the boil. Pour this slowly over the cornflour mix, stirring all the time. Clean the pan, then pour the milk mixture and vanilla pod back into it. Cook over a medium heat, stirring all the time, until it just comes to the boil and is thick enough to coat the back of a spoon.

3 Remove from the heat, stir in the crème fraîche, then pour into a bowl. Place a piece of clingfilm over the surface to prevent a skin forming, then leave to cool. Chill in the fridge until really cold, for at least 4–5 hours but preferably overnight.

4 Remove the vanilla pod from the custard, then transfer the custard to a jug. Turn on the ice-cream machine, then slowly pour in the custard. Leave to churn for 10–30 minutes (depending on your machine). When it stops, spoon into a plastic container, cover with clingfilm and a lid, then freeze for at least 3–4 hours. (If you don't have an ice-cream machine, pour the custard into a strong plastic container and freeze for several hours, stirring with a fork once an hour. This will help to give a smoother texture. When almost frozen, freeze for at least 3–4 hours.)

5 For the best results, soften in the fridge for 1–1½ hours before serving. Serve with the raspberries. It will keep for up to 1 month. Do not re-freeze.

use fewer egg yolks and eliminate double cream to reduce the fat and introduce half-fat crème fraîche, custard powder and cornflour

Chocolate mousse

This sophisticated dessert is great for a dinner party. To serve as a lighter family pud, you could use an ordinary dark chocolate with a lower percentage of cocoa solids (about 40–50%), although this will make each serving higher in sugar. This is a favourite for chocaholics, with less than half the fat of a classic recipe.

	Classic	Lighter
Kcals	397	167
Fat	29 g	10 g
Sat fat	14 g	5 g
Sugar	20 g	11 g

Per serving 167 kcals

Protein 4 g, carbs 15g, fat 10 g,
sat fat 5g, fibre 2 g, sugar 11 g, salt 0.12 g

Serves 4

Prep: 20 minutes, plus cooling
and chilling

85 g (3 oz) dark chocolate, 70% cocoa solids

1 tablespoon cocoa powder, plus extra for dusting

½ teaspoon instant coffee granules

½ teaspoon vanilla extract

2 medium egg whites

1 tablespoon golden caster sugar

50 g (2 oz) full-fat Greek yogurt

fresh raspberries, to decorate

1 Chop the chocolate very finely and put it into a large heatproof bowl that will fit over a pan of simmering water. Mix the cocoa, coffee and vanilla with 2 tablespoons cold water, and pour over the chocolate. Place the bowl over the gently simmering water, give it all a stir, then remove from the heat. Leave with the bowl of chocolate still over the water, stirring occasionally to check when melted.

2 Stir the melted chocolate – it will be quite thick. Stir in 2 tablespoons boiling water and the chocolate will immediately thin down and become silky smooth. Leave to cool slightly.

3 In a mixing bowl, whisk the egg whites to fairly soft peaks, then whisk in the sugar until thick and glossy.

4 Beat the yogurt into the cooled chocolate. Fold about one-third of the egg whites into the chocolate mix using a large metal spoon, then very gently fold in the rest of the whites until they are evenly mixed in – being careful not to over mix or you will lose the volume of the mousse. Spoon into 4 small cups or 125–150 ml (4–5 fl oz) ramekins and chill for a couple of hours, or overnight.

5 Place each mousse on a saucer or small plate. Top with a few raspberries, then dust with a little cocoa powder. Will keep for up to 2 days in the fridge.

Reduce fat by eliminating egg yolks, butter and cream and by replacing a little of the chocolate with cocoa powder and using Greek yogurt

Apple and blackberry crumble

Like many desserts that are full of fruit, the ever-popular crumble can seem like a healthy option, but it has other ingredients that are high in fat and sugar. By making a few simple changes that don't compromise the taste, the sugar and fat have been lowered considerably.

	Classic	Lighter
Kcals	493	353
Fat	21.6 g	11.9 g
Sat fat	9.5 g	3.2 g
Sugar	45.1 g	33.7 g

Per serving 353 kcals

Protein 5.9 g, carbs 54.1 g, fat 11.9 g, sat fat 3.2 g, fibre 6.5 g, sugar 33.7 g, salt 0.1g

Serves 5

Prep: 35 minutes
Cook: 35 minutes

For the crumble

85 g (3 oz) plain flour

3 tablespoons ground almonds

50 g (2 oz) porridge oats (not jumbo)

25 g (1 oz) butter, at soft room temperature, cut into pieces

3 tablespoons golden caster sugar

1 teaspoon ground cinnamon

1 tablespoon chopped, toasted hazelnuts

1½ tablespoons rapeseed oil

For the fruit

2 oranges

1 tablespoon demerara sugar

800 g (1 lb 12 oz) eating apples, such as Braeburn or Cox's, peeled, cored and chopped into small chunks

175 g (6 oz) fresh blackberries

1 tablespoon cornflour

1 Make the crumble topping. Put the flour, ground almonds, oats and butter in a mixing bowl. Rub the butter in with your fingertips to create quite rough breadcrumbs. Stir in the sugar, cinnamon and hazelnuts, then stir in the oil and mix in with your fingers to evenly distribute. Set aside. Preheat the oven to 190°C (fan 170°C/375°F/gas mark 5).

2 Finely grate 1 teaspoon zest from one of the oranges and set aside, then squeeze the juice from both to give you 100 ml (3½ fl oz) juice. Make up with water if necessary. Put the orange juice and sugar in a saucepan and simmer for about 1 minute to dissolve the sugar and make it a bit syrupy.

3 Tip in the apples, reserved orange zest and 4 tablespoons water, then simmer for 5 minutes or until the apples are only just starting to soften (they will finish cooking in the oven). Stir in the blackberries and simmer for another 1–2 minutes to release their juices and colour the liquid. Stir in the cornflour, letting the mixture bubble briefly to thicken and make a sauce. Adjust with a little extra water if you want the saucy bit any thinner.

4 Spoon the fruit into an ovenproof dish about 25 x 20 x 5 cm (10 x 8 x 2 inches) and scatter over the topping but do not press it down; keep it light and crumbly. Bake for about 25 minutes or until the topping is golden and the fruit and its juices are bubbling up around the edges. Remove and leave to settle for 10–15 minutes before serving.

create flavour and crunch in the crumble with cinnamon and a few nuts instead of extra sugar. To improve fibre content, include oats to replace some of the flour

Semifreddo with summer fruits

To ensure the texture of this delicious dessert isn't lost, I've adapted both method and ingredients to recreate that same sense of luxurious richness, but in a much lighter way.

	Classic	Lighter
Kcals	322	162
Fat	27.5 g	9 g
Sat fat	15.7 g	5.6 g
Sugar	15 g	13.9 g

Per serving 162 kcals

Protein 4.4 g, carbs 15.7 g, fat 9 g, sat fat 5.6 g, fibre 1.8 g, sugar 13.9 g, salt 0.1g

Serves 8

Prep: 30 minutes, plus cooling, chilling and freezing
Cook: 8 minutes

50 g (2 oz) golden caster sugar

1½ teaspoons custard powder

1½ teaspoons cornflour

250 ml (9 fl oz) full-fat milk

1 large egg yolk

200 ml (7 fl oz) half-fat crème fraîche

¼ teaspoon vanilla extract

250 g (9 oz) Greek yogurt

450 g (1 lb) frozen summer berries, such as redcurrants and blackcurrants, and small berries such as strawberries, raspberries and blackberries

2 teaspoons icing sugar

1 Mix the sugar, custard powder and cornflour in a mixing bowl with 2 tablespoons of the milk. Beat in the egg yolk. Pour the rest of the milk into a saucepan and bring just to the boil. Pour the hot milk slowly over the cornflour mix, stirring constantly. Pour this into a clean pan, preferably non-stick, and cook over a medium heat, stirring all the time with a wooden spoon, until the mixture comes just to the boil, thickens and coats the back of the spoon – about 5 minutes. Remove from the heat, stir in the crème fraîche and vanilla and pour into a bowl. Cover with a piece of clingfilm and leave to cool. When it's cooled down, put in the fridge and leave overnight.

2 Line the base of a 1 kg (2 lb 4 oz) loaf tin, about 22 x 13 x 6 cm (8½ x 5 x 2½ inches), with baking parchment. Spoon the cold custard into a food processor with the yogurt and 300 g (11 oz) of the frozen fruit. Process briefly to combine everything and break down the fruit a bit. It's important that the fruit is still frozen, as this will also start to freeze the whole mixture. Pour or spoon the mix into the lined tin, cover and put in the freezer for about 6 hours. Tip the rest of the fruit into a sieve set over a small bowl and leave to thaw and drain.

3 When the rest of the fruit has thawed, set a small handful of the fruit aside for decoration and press the rest through the sieve to make a fruit coulis. Stir in the icing sugar to sweeten. (If your mix of fruit is quite tart, you may need a pinch more icing sugar.) Keep in the fridge until ready to serve.

4 To serve, when the semifreddo feels firm enough to turn out but not completely solid, loosen the edges with a small palette knife (or dip the tin briefly in hot water to loosen the sides first if that's easier), then turn it out on to a serving plate and peel off the lining paper. Scatter the whole fruits down the centre and spoon a little of the coulis over them. Serve in slices with the rest of the coulis.

Lower the fat by reducing the number of eggs and create texture by making a lower-fat custard instead

Bread and butter pudding

This traditional British pudding has become richer over the years as well as more fattening. So I've reinvented it to make it lighter by a careful choice of ingredients and using a good amount of fruit.

	Classic	Lighter
Kcals	569	312
Fat	33.8 g	11.5 g
Sat fat	18.1 g	6.1 g
Sugar	33.3 g	19.8 g

Per serving 312 kcals

Protein 9.6 g, carbs 40.9 g, fat 11.5 g, sat fat 6.1 g, fibre 1.7 g, sugar 19.8 g, salt 0.83 g

Serves 4

Prep: 25 minutes, plus soaking and infusing
Cook: 30–35 minutes

50 g (2 oz) soft dried apricots, chopped

25 g (1 oz) raisins

2 tablespoons brandy

1 large egg

1 teaspoon golden caster sugar

2 teaspoons custard powder

350 ml (12 fl oz) semi-skimmed milk

½ vanilla pod, slit lengthways

zest of 1 small lemon, pared off in strips with a vegetable peeler

4 tablespoons half-fat crème fraîche

25 g (1 oz) butter, at room temperature

4 medium slices good white bread, crusts left on, such as sliced from a small white farmhouse loaf

1 tablespoon apricot conserve or jam

¼ teaspoon sifted icing sugar, for dusting

1 Put the apricots and raisins in a small dish, pour over the brandy and leave to soak, stirring occasionally.

2 Meanwhile, beat the egg and caster sugar together in a mixing bowl, then whisk in the custard powder until smooth. Warm the milk in a small, non-stick saucepan, then, when it's just coming up to the boil, remove from the heat and slowly stir into the egg mixture. Scrape in the vanilla seeds, add the lemon zest and vanilla pod and set aside to cool and infuse for 30 minutes. Whisk the crème fraîche into the cooled custard, then strain into a jug.

3 Using ¼ teaspoon of the butter, very lightly butter a shallow ovenproof dish, about 20 x 25 x 5 cm (8 x 10 x 2 inches).

4 Butter the bread on one side only with the rest of the butter, then spread over the conserve or jam. Cut each slice into 4 triangles, then lay half the triangles, jam-side up, in the dish. Scatter over half of the apricots and raisins, then lay the rest of the bread over the top, jam-side up. Scatter over the rest of the dried fruit and any unsoaked brandy, then pour half of the custard over the bread. Leave to soak for 15 minutes. Preheat the oven to 180°C (fan 160°C/350°F/gas mark 4).

5 Place the dish in a roasting tin. Pour the rest of the custard over the bread, press the bread lightly into the custard, then half-fill the roasting tin with hot water. Bake for 20 minutes, then increase the oven temperature to 190°C (fan 170°C/375°F/gas mark 5) and bake for a further 5–10 minutes until the bread on top is crisp and golden. Remove and let the pudding sit for 2–3 minutes. Dust over the icing sugar and serve warm.

use semi-skimmed milk instead of full-fat, and half-fat crème fraîche instead of cream. Maintain the flavour by adding lemon, vanilla and brandy

Strawberry ice cream milk shake

It's hard to refuse a cool, frothy milkshake on a hot day, especially with the added allure of scoops of rich vanilla ice cream whizzed through it. But with this allure comes lots of fat and sugar. If you keep a batch of the Vanilla Ice Cream (see p. 144) in the freezer, it's quick to whisk these up as an equally alluring, but low-fat, dessert alternative.

	Classic	Lighter
Kcals	408	196
Fat	19.2 g	7.7 g
Sat fat	12 g	4.6 g
Sugar	47 g	22.8 g

Per glass 196 kcals

Protein 7.7 g, carbs 23.6 g, fat 7.7 g, sat fat 4.6 g, fibre 1.8 g, sugar 22.8 g, salt 0.2g

Fills 2 tall glasses

Prep: 10 minutes (not including making the ice cream)

250 g (9 oz) ripe fresh strawberries, hulled and halved, or quartered if large

200 ml (7 fl oz) semi-skimmed milk

2 tablespoons natural yogurt

2 scoops Vanilla Ice Cream (see recipe p. 144)

1 Put the strawberries in a blender or food processor (or use a stick hand blender) with the milk, yogurt and ice cream, then process until the mixture is creamy and frothy.

2 Pour into 2 tall glasses and spoon the frothy bubbles on top.

Eliminate sugar by using ripe, seasonal strawberries when they are at their natural sweetest

Raspberry and passion fruit pavlova

I've tweaked the size of the meringue, generously filled it with lower fat creaminess and now this recipe is lower in sugar and dramatically lower in fat and calories – yet it still looks and tastes like an indulgence.

	Classic	Lighter
Kcals	326	180
Fat	20.3 g	7.3 g
Sat fat	12.6 g	4.6 g
Sugar	33 g	23.3 g

Per serving 180 kcals
Protein 4.8 g, carbs 23.5 g, fat 7.3 g, sat fat 4.6g, fibre 1.5g, sugar 23.3g, salt 0.1g

Serves 8
Prep: 25 minutes, plus drying out
Cook: 1 hour

For the meringue
1 teaspoon cornflour

1 teaspoon white wine vinegar

½ teaspoon vanilla extract

3 large egg whites

100 g (4 oz) golden caster sugar

50 g (2 oz) icing sugar

For the filling
100 ml (3½ fl oz) whipping cream

200 g (7 oz) 2% Greek yogurt

85 g (3 oz) half-fat crème fraîche

2 teaspoons golden caster sugar

1 passion fruit

350 g (12 oz) fresh raspberries

1 Preheat the oven to 150°C (fan 130°C/300°F/gas mark 2). Line a large baking sheet with baking parchment and draw a 20 cm (8 inch) circle in pencil in the centre of the paper. For the meringue, mix together the cornflour, vinegar and vanilla and set aside.

2 Whisk the egg whites in a large mixing bowl until the mixture stands in stiff peaks when the blades are lifted. Start to add the caster sugar a tablespoon at a time, beating for a few seconds before adding the next tablespoon. When all the caster sugar has been added you should have a thick, glossy mixture. Now sift and gently fold in half of the icing sugar using a large metal spoon. Repeat with the remaining icing sugar, being careful not to overmix. Fold in the cornflour mixture.

3 Spoon and gently spread the mixture into the circle on the baking parchment, building the sides up slightly so that they are just a bit higher. Bake for 1 hour, after which the meringue should sound crisp when gently tapped. Turn the oven off, but leave the meringue in to finish drying out as it cools, for another 1 hour. Don't worry if it cracks a bit – it's part of its character.

4 When ready to serve, remove the merigue case from the baking parchment and place on a serving plate. Whisk the whipping cream for the filling to soft peaks, enough so that it holds its shape. Fold in the yogurt, then the crème fraîche and sugar. Cut the passion fruit in half widthways, scoop out the pulp and seeds from one half and lightly ripple through the creamy mix. Spoon this into the meringue case. Scatter the raspberries on top, drizzling the remaining passion fruit over as you go. Serve straight away. If left filled for too long, the meringue will start to soften.

Replace most of the cream with 2% Greek yogurt and half-fat crème fraîche, to greatly reduce fat

Crème brûlée

A winning dessert, this crème brûlée cheats on fat content by using single cream instead of double and a custard with fewer eggs. The secret to this healthier version is to make sure the custard is made very thick initially, as unlike your classic crème brûlée recipe, the custard isn't baked afterwards.

	Classic	Lighter
Kcals	700	257
Fat	65.1 g	14.9 g
Sat fat	38.1 g	8.7 g
Sugar	22 g	18.9 g

Per serving 257 kcals

Protein 5.2 g, carbs 25.3 g, fat 14.9 g, sat fat 8.7 g, sugar 18.9 g, salt 0.2 g

Serves 4

Prep: 15 minutes, plus cooling and chilling
Cook: 25 minutes

4 tablespoons golden caster sugar

1 tablespoon custard powder

1 tablespoon cornflour

200 ml (7 fl oz) semi-skimmed milk

2 large egg yolks

125 ml (4 fl oz) single cream

1 vanilla pod

140 g (5 oz) half-fat créme fraîche

1 Mix 2 tablespoons of the sugar, the custard powder and the cornflour in a mixing bowl with 2 tablespoons of the milk to make a smooth paste. Beat the egg yolks in well with a fork.

2 Pour the rest of the milk into a saucepan, preferably non-stick, then pour in the cream. Slit the vanilla pod lengthways and scrape the vanilla seeds into the milk. Drop the pod into the pan and bring the creamy milk just to the boil. Remove from the heat as soon as you see a few bubbles rising to the surface.

3 Slowly pour and stir the hot milk into the cornflour mix, including the vanilla pod, making sure the yolks are well blended in. Transfer to a clean pan. Cook over a low heat, stirring all the time with a wooden spoon, for 12–15 minutes until the mixture is very thick. When you drag the spoon across the bottom of the pan, it should leave a clean line. The mixture should have thickened after 10 minutes, but keep stirring until it has thickened sufficiently to look like softly whipped cream or mayonnaise. Keep adjusting the heat to prevent the mixture coming to the boil or overheating, as it may curdle and become lumpy. If this should happen, beat smooth with a wire whisk.

4 Remove from the heat and leave to cool for 15–20 minutes, stirring occasionally to prevent a skin from forming. Remove the vanilla pod. Stir in the créme fraîche and spoon the mixture into 4 small (150 ml/¼ pint) ramekins. Spread the mixture level, then chill, uncovered, for 4 hours or overnight. By not covering them, a thin skin can form on top of the brûlées, which will help support the caramel layer later.

5 When ready to serve, spoon the remaining sugar over the top of each brûlée (allow 1½ teaspoons per ramekin) and smooth it over with the back of the spoon. To caramelize it, use a kitchen blow torch. Hold the flame just above the sugar and keep it moving round and round until evenly caramelized, but not too long or the custard will heat up too much. Serve straight away while the caramel is firm and brittle, as it will soften on standing.

make a thick custard that does not require as many egg yolks to set as it would if baked

Sticky toffee pudding

This pudding is all about excess and naughtiness – but I've discovered that you really don't need all that butter, cream, syrup, sugar and treacle to make it taste gorgeous.

	Classic	Lighter
Kcals	699	450
Fat	36 g	17.5 g
Sat fat	20.7 g	4.6 g
Sugar	74.4 g	49.8 g

Per serving 450 kcals

Protein 6 g, carbs 70.6 g, fat 17.5 g, sat fat 4.6 g, fibre 2 g, sugar 49.8 g, salt 0.79 g.

Makes 7

Prep: 35 minutes, plus cooling
Cook: 20–25 minutes

For the puddings

200 g (7 oz) pitted whole medjool dates

1 teaspoon vanilla extract

1 teaspoon black treacle

2 medium eggs

1 teaspoon bicarbonate of soda

175 g (6 oz) self-raising flour, plus extra for dusting

75 ml (2½ fl oz) rapeseed oil, plus ½ teaspoon for greasing

100 g (4 oz) demerara sugar

100 g (4 oz) natural yogurt

For the toffee sauce

100 g (4 oz) light muscovado sugar

25 g (1 oz) butter, cut into pieces

1½ teaspoons black treacle

1½ teaspoons vanilla extract

100 g (4 oz) half-fat crème fraîche

1 Chop the dates, put them in a small bowl, then pour over 175 ml (6 fl oz) boiling water. Leave to cool for about 30 minutes. Grease 7 x 200 ml (7 fl oz) pudding tins with ½ teaspoon oil, then flour and place on a baking sheet.

2 Stir the vanilla and treacle into the dates, and mash with a fork to a rough purée.

3 Preheat the oven to 180°C (fan 160°C/350° F/gas mark 4). To make the puddings, beat the eggs in a small bowl. Mix the bicarbonate of soda and 175 g (6 oz) flour together. Stir the 75 ml (2½ fl oz) oil and the sugar together in a larger mixing bowl, using a wooden spoon. Pour in the eggs a bit at a time, beating as you go. Gently fold in one-third of the flour mixture with a large metal spoon, then half of the yogurt. Don't overmix. Repeat, finishing with the last of the flour. Gently stir in the mashed dates in to form a thick batter. Spoon the batter evenly between the tins. Bake for 20–25 minutes.

4 Meanwhile, make the sauce. Put the sugar and butter into a small, heavy-based pan. Heat over a low-medium heat, stirring occasionally, until the sugar starts to dissolve, without bringing to the boil. The mixture will be quite thick and the sugar won't dissolve completely at this stage. Take the pan off the heat, then stir in the treacle and vanilla. Cool for 1–2 minutes, then stir in the crème fraîche a spoonful at a time. Use a small wire whisk to make the mixture smooth if necessary.

5 To serve, loosen around the sides of the puddings with a round-bladed knife, then turn out on to plates. Spoon and drizzle a little sauce over and around each one.

Reduce the sugar and concentrate the flavour by using unrefined sugar and black treacle, together with vanilla extract

GUILT-FREE BAKING

Carrot cake

Although this North American classic is plumped up with freshly grated carrot and blended with oil instead of butter, it's not enough to warrant the healthy tag unless you adjust the ingredients and techniques.

	Classic	Lighter
Kcals	327	217
Fat	20.5 g	9 g
Sat fat	5.5 g	1 g
Sugar	21.5 g	21 g

Per square 217 kcals

Protein 4 g, carbs 31 g, fat 9 g, sat fat 1 g, fibre 2 g, sugar 21 g, salt 0.52 g

Cuts into 16 squares

Prep: 30 minutes, plus soaking
Cook: 1 hour

For the cake

1 medium orange

140 g (5 oz) raisins

115 g (4 oz) self-raising flour

115 g (4 oz) plain wholemeal flour

1 teaspoon baking powder, plus a pinch

1 teaspoon bicarbonate of soda

1 teaspoon ground cinnamon

2 large eggs

140 g (5 oz) dark muscovado sugar

125 ml (4 fl oz) rapeseed oil, plus extra for greasing

280 g (10 oz) carrot, finely grated

For the frosting

100 g (4 oz) light soft cheese, chilled

100 g (4 oz) quark cheese

3 tablespoons sifted icing sugar

½ teaspoon finely grated orange zest

1½ teaspoons lemon juice

1 Preheat the oven to 160°C (fan 140°C/325°F/gas mark 3). Lightly grease the base of a deep 20 cm (8 inch) square cake tin with rapeseed oil, then line the base with baking parchment.

2 To make the cake, finely grate the zest from the orange and squeeze 3 tablespoons of the juice. Pour the juice over the raisins in a bowl, stir in the zest, then leave to soak. Mix the flours with the 1 teaspoon baking powder, bicarbonate of soda and the cinnamon.

3 Separate one of the eggs. Put the white in a small bowl and the yolk in a large mixing bowl. Break the remaining egg in with the yolk, then tip in the sugar. Whisk together for 1–2 minutes until thick and foamy. Slowly pour in the oil and continue to whisk on a low speed until well mixed. Tip in the flour mix, half at a time, and gently stir it into the egg mixture. The mix will be quite stiff. Put the extra pinch of baking powder in with the egg white and whisk to soft peaks.

4 Fold the carrot and raisins (with any liquid) into the flour mixture. Gently fold in the whisked egg white, then pour into the tin. Jiggle the tin to level the mixture. Bake for 1 hour until risen and firm or until a skewer inserted in the centre comes out clean. Leave to cool in the tin for 5 minutes, turn out on to a wire rack, peel off the lining paper, then leave until cold.

5 To make the frosting, stir the soft cheese, quark, icing sugar and orange zest together – don't overbeat. Stir in the lemon juice. Swirl the frosting over the cake and cut into 16 squares. This cake is even better if left for a day or two, well wrapped, before icing.

use rapeseed oil, light soft cheese and quark to lower the fats. Reduce sugar in the frosting, and add flavour with oranges and lemons

Chocolate brownies

A brownie can appear in many guises – plump and gooey, nutty, cakey or fudgy. But it is always exceedingly rich with a thin, crusty top and dark, chewy centre. As this is achieved by mixing together generous combinations of butter, sugar, chocolate and eggs, my challenge was to create a lighter version that was still irresistible.

	Classic	Lighter
Kcals	314	191
Fat	19 g	11 g
Sat fat	10 g	3 g
Sugar	25.6 g	16 g

Per square 191 kcals

Protein 2 g, carbs 23 g, fat 11 g, sat fat 3 g, fibre 1 g, sugar 16 g, salt 0.28 g

Cuts into 12 squares

Prep: 25 minutes
Cook: 35 minutes

85 g (3 oz) dark chocolate, 70% cocoa solids, chopped into small pieces

rapeseed oil, for greasing

85 g (3 oz) plain flour

25 g (1 oz) cocoa powder

¼ teaspoon bicarbonate of soda

100 g (4 oz) golden caster sugar

50 g (2 oz) light muscovado sugar

½ teaspoon instant coffee granules

1 teaspoon vanilla extract

2 tablespoons buttermilk

1 large egg

100 g (4 oz) mayonnaise

1. Preheat the oven to 180°C (fan 160°C/350°F/gas mark 4). Pour enough water into a small pan to one-third fill it. Bring to the boil, then remove the pan from the heat. Put the chopped chocolate into a large heatproof bowl that will fit snugly over the pan without touching the water. Sit the pan over the water (still off the heat) and leave the chocolate to melt slowly for a few minutes, stirring occasionally until it has melted evenly. Remove the bowl from the pan, then let the chocolate cool slightly.

2. Meanwhile, lightly grease a 19 cm (7½ inch) square, 5 cm (2 inches) deep, cake tin with the rapeseed oil, then line the base with baking parchment. Sift together the flour, cocoa and bicarbonate of soda. Using a wooden spoon, stir both the sugars into the cooled chocolate with the coffee, vanilla and buttermilk. Stir in 1 tablespoon warm water. Break and beat in the egg, then stir in the mayonnaise just until smooth and glossy. Sift over the flour and cocoa mix, then gently fold in with a spatula without overmixing.

3. Pour the mixture into the tin, then gently and evenly spread it into the corners. Bake for 30 minutes. When a skewer is inserted into the middle, it should come out with just a few moist crumbs sticking to it. If cooked too long, the mix will dry out; not long enough and it can sink. Leave in the tin until completely cold, then loosen the sides with a round-bladed knife. Turn out on to a board, peel off the lining paper and cut into 12 squares.

Reduce the fat by replacing all the butter and some of the egg with mayonnaise. Use good-quality chocolate so that you can use less, and intensify the chocolate taste with cocoa powder and coffee granules

Coffee and walnut cake

Walnuts contain a good fat, but they are fattening in terms of calories, so this cake uses alternatives to boost the taste. I've also used coffee syrup livened up with a splash of vanilla to deepen the coffee experience, and abandoned the traditional cake-making method for one that allows me to lighten this tea-time favourite.

	Classic	Lighter
Kcals	462	336
Fat	27 g	15 g
Sat fat	13 g	4 g
Sugar	42 g	30 g

Per slice 336 kcals

Protein 8 g, carbs 45 g, fat 15 g, sat fat 4 g, fibre 1 g, sugar 30 g, salt 0.43 g

Cuts into 12 slices

Prep: 30 minutes, plus cooling and setting
Cook: 45–50 minutes

For the cake

1 tablespoon instant coffee granules, plus 1 teaspoon

225 g (8 oz) self-raising flour

1 teaspoon baking powder

50 g (2 oz) ground almonds

85 g (3 oz) light muscovado sugar

50 g (2 oz) golden caster sugar

25 g (1 oz) chopped walnuts

2 large eggs, beaten

250 g (9 oz) natural yogurt

75 ml (2½ fl oz) walnut oil, plus extra for greasing

For the filling

2 tablespoons golden caster sugar

2 teaspoons instant coffee granules

140 g (5 oz) light mascarpone cheese

100 g (4 oz) quark cheese

1 tablespoon sifted icing sugar

¼ teaspoon vanilla extract

For the icing

140 g (5 oz) fondant icing sugar

1 teaspoon instant coffee granules

1 tablespoon finely chopped walnuts

1 Preheat the oven to 180°C (fan 160°C/350°F/gas mark 4). Lightly oil a 20 cm (8 inch) round, 6 cm (2½ inch) deep, loose-bottomed cake tin with walnut oil, then line the base with parchment paper.

2 For the cake, mix the coffee with 2 teaspoons warm water and set aside. Tip the flour into a large mixing bowl. Stir in the baking powder, ground almonds, both sugars and walnuts, then make a well in the centre. Put the eggs, yogurt, oil and coffee mix into the well and stir the mixture with a wooden spoon so that everything is evenly mixed.

3 Spoon the mixture into the prepared tin, smooth the top to level it, then bake for 40–45 minutes, or until a skewer inserted into the centre of the cake comes out clean. Let the cake cool in the tin briefly, then turn it out and peel off the lining paper. Place on a wire rack to cool completely while you make the filling and icing.

4 Make the syrup for the filling. Put the caster sugar and coffee into a small, heavy-based saucepan, then pour in 3 tablespoons water. Heat gently, stirring to help the sugar dissolve. Once dissolved, raise the heat, then boil at a fast rolling boil for about 2½–3 minutes until thickened and syrupy. Pour into a small heatproof bowl and set aside to cool. When cold it should be the consistency of treacle.

5 Meanwhile, beat the mascarpone, quark, icing sugar and vanilla together until smooth, then stir in the cold coffee syrup. Set aside.

6 For the icing, sift the fondant icing sugar into a bowl. Mix the coffee with the 1 tablespoon warm water, then stir this into the icing sugar with the extra water to give a smooth, thick but spreadable icing.

7 Split the cake into 3, then sandwich back together with the filling. Spread the icing over the top, scatter over the chopped walnuts and leave to set. Store in the fridge.

Replace butter in the cake with walnut oil and yogurt to reduce the fat and saturated fat

•

Replace a buttercream filling with one made with light mascarpone and quark to reduce the fat further

•

Reduce walnuts and gain walnut flavour from the oil

•

Use less sugar in the cake - bump up the flavour by combining light muscovado with golden caster. Make a filling that requires less sugar

Treacle tart

With less than half the sugar of a classic treacle tart, this recipe is bound to impress. By finding ways to reduce the syrup, this is the perfect way to finish a Sunday lunch that is far less heavy on the calories. Serve the tart while still warm and, if there is any left, it is equally lovely cold.

	Classic	Lighter
Kcals	469	247
Fat	14.8 g	10.2 g
Sat fat	8.7 g	3.9 g
Sugar	47.9 g	20.1 g

Per slice 247 kcals

Protein 3.6 g, carbs 34.7 g, fat 10.2 g, sat fat 3.9 g, fibre 1.1 g, sugar 20.1 g, salt 0.5 g

Serves 8

Prep: 15 minutes, plus chilling and standing
Cook: 50 minutes

For the base

225 g (8 oz) bought shortcrust pastry

plain flour for dusting

For the filling

1 medium egg

3 tablespoons half-fat crème fraîche

175 g (6 oz) golden syrup

1 tablespoon black treacle

1 small eating apple, such as Cox's (140 g/5 oz total weight), cored, peeled and coarsely grated

50 g (2 oz) fresh white breadcrumbs

1 lemon

1 Preheat the oven to 200°C (fan 180°C/400°F/gas mark 6). Roll the pastry out thinly on a lightly floured surface and use to line a 23 cm (9 inch) round, 2.5 cm (1 inch) deep, fluted flan tin, easing the pastry into the tin and the flutes carefully to prevent it stretching. Run a rolling pin over the top of the tin to trim off any excess pastry. Prick the pastry base lightly with a fork. Chill for 10 minutes while the oven heats up.

2 Place the flan tin on a baking sheet. Line the pastry with foil and baking beans and bake for 12 minutes until the pastry is set. Remove the foil and beans from the pastry case and bake for another 5 minutes until the pastry is very pale golden. Remove and lower the oven temperature to 180°C (fan 160°C/350°F/gas mark 4).

3 While the pastry is baking, make the filling. Beat the egg in a mixing bowl, then stir in the crème fraîche, golden syrup, treacle, grated apple and breadcrumbs. Finely grate the zest from the lemon and stir it into the filling. Mix with 1 tablespoon of squeezed lemon juice. Leave to stand for 10–15 minutes so that the bread can absorb the other ingredients slightly.

4 Pour the filling into the pastry case and bake for 30 minutes or until the filling is softly set. Remove the tart and let it cool a little to firm up. Remove from the tin and serve.

Reduce sugar by replacing some of the syrup with grated apple, and using a medium egg and half-fat crème fraîche to provide bulk and texture

Lemon drizzle cake

A moist, fragrant slice of lemon drizzle cake is a classic tea-time treat. For this healthier version I've made a butterless cake and added lots of lemon zest to the mixture for a really zingy taste.

	Classic	Lighter
Kcals	335	243
Fat	17.9 g	10.2 g
Sat fat	10.4 g	1.4 g
Sugar	27.6 g	21.5 g

Per slice 243 kcals

Protein 4.7 g, carbs 35.4 g, fat 10.2 g, sat fat 1.4 g, fibre 0.9 g, sugar 21.5 g, salt 0.34 g

Cuts into 12 slices

Prep: 25 minutes
Cook: 40 minutes

For the cake

175 g (6 oz) self-raising flour

1½ teaspoons baking powder

50 g (2 oz) ground almonds

50 g (2 oz) polenta

finely grated zest of 2 lemons

140 g (5 oz) golden caster sugar

2 large eggs

225 g (8 oz) natural yogurt

75 ml (2½ fl oz) rapeseed oil, plus extra for greasing

For the syrup

85 g (3 oz) golden caster sugar

juice of 2 lemons (about 5 tablespoons)

1 Preheat the oven to 180°C (fan 160°C/350°F/gas mark 4). Lightly grease a 20 cm (8 inch) round, 5 cm (2 inch) deep cake tin with rapeseed oil, then line the base with baking parchment.

2 For the cake, put the flour, baking powder, ground almonds and polenta in a large mixing bowl. Stir in the lemon zest and sugar, then make a well in the centre. Beat the eggs in a bowl, then stir in the yogurt. Tip this mixture along with the oil into the well, then briefly and gently stir with a large metal spoon so that everything is just combined, without overmixing.

3 Spoon the mixture into the tin and level the top. Bake for 40 minutes or until a skewer inserted into the centre of the cake comes out clean. Cover loosely with foil for the final 5–10 minutes if it starts to brown too quickly.

4 While the cake cooks, make the lemon syrup. Tip the sugar into a small saucepan with the lemon juice and 75 ml (2½ fl oz) water. Heat over a medium heat, stirring occasionally, until the sugar has dissolved. Raise the heat, boil for 4 minutes until slightly reduced and syrupy, then remove from the heat.

5 Remove the cake from the oven and let it cool briefly in the tin. While it is still warm, turn it out of the tin, peel off the lining paper and sit the cake on a wire rack set over a baking sheet or plate. Use a skewer to make lots of small holes all over the top of the cake. Slowly spoon over half of the lemon syrup and let it soak in. Spoon over the rest in the same way, brushing the edges and sides of the cake too with the last of the syrup.

Mix in ground almonds to lighten and moisten, and bulk out with polenta, which intensifies the texture and colour

Sticky gingerbread

Most people's favourite kind of gingerbread is moist, sticky and dark. To gain these qualities, lots of butter, sugar, syrup and milk is involved. Here, I've kept the characteristics with less fat and sugar. If you keep the cake well wrapped for a day before cutting, you'll find it gets even stickier.

	Classic	Lighter
Kcals	162	130
Fat	6.9 g	4 g
Sat fat	4 g	1.1 g
Sugar	13 g	11 g

Per square 130 kcals

Protein 2.3 g, carbs 21.1 g, fat 4 g, sat fat 1.1 g, fibre 0.6 g, sugar 11 g, salt 0.3g

Cuts into 16 squares

Prep: 25 minutes, plus cooling
Cook: about 55 minutes

140 g (5 oz) dried pitted whole dates, chopped into small pieces

25 g (1 oz) butter

85 g (3 oz) black treacle

25 g (1 oz) golden syrup

3 tablespoons rapeseed oil, plus extra for greasing tin

1 large egg

150 ml (¼ pint) buttermilk

225 g (8 oz) plain flour

1 teaspoon bicarbonate of soda

3½ teaspoons ground ginger

½ teaspoon ground cinnamon

50 g (2 oz) dark muscovado sugar

1 Put the dates in a small bowl, then pour over 125 ml (4 fl oz) boiling water. Leave to cool for 30 minutes. Lightly grease a 20 cm (8 inch) square, 5 cm (2 inches) deep, cake tin with rapeseed oil, then line the base with baking parchment.

2 Measure the butter into a small pan with the treacle and syrup. Put over a low heat to melt the butter, then remove and pour in the oil. Set aside. Preheat the oven to 160°C (fan 140°C/325°F/gas mark 3).

3 Blend the dates and their liquid in a mini blender or small food processor to a thick purée. Beat the egg in a small bowl and stir in the buttermilk. Mix the flour with the bicarbonate of soda, ginger, cinnamon and sugar. Pour the egg, the date and the treacle mixtures into the bowl with the flour mixture and beat briefly together with a wooden spoon just until well mixed. The mixture will be soft like a thick batter. Pour it into the lined tin, level the mixture and bake for about 50–55 minutes. To test if done, insert a skewer in the centre. If the skewer comes out clean with no uncooked mixture on it, and the cake feels firm but springy to the touch, it should be done.

4 Leave in the tin for a few minutes before removing to a wire rack, peeling off the lining paper and leaving to cool completely. Wrap well and, if you like, leave for a day before slicing for it to become even stickier. It will keep for up to 1 week.

Let the dates provide some of the stickiness, instead of relying on all sugar and syrup. Replace milk and most of the butter with buttermilk and rapeseed oil to lower fat and saturated fat

Banana bread

For such an easy mix cake, this fruity bake packs loads of flavour. With that, however, comes a lot of sugar, fat and saturated fat. While cutting back on these, I've found ways to still keep its sweet butteriness.

	Classic	Lighter
Kcals	290	194
Fat	16.6 g	8.5 g
Sat fat	6.8 g	2 g
Sugar	17 g	11.4 g

Per slice 194 kcals

Protein 4.3 g, carbs 24.7 g, fat 8.5 g, sat fat 2 g, fibre 1.4 g, sugar 11.4g, salt 0.3g

Cuts into 12 slices

Prep: 25 minutes
Cook: 50–55 minutes

2 very ripe medium bananas, preferably with black skins

finely grated zest of ½ lemon

½ teaspoon vanilla extract

175 g (6 oz) plain flour

50 g (2 oz) plain wholemeal flour

1½ teaspoons baking powder

½ teaspoon bicarbonate of soda

25 g (1 oz) ground almonds

25 g (1 oz) butter, at soft room temperature, cut into pieces

85 g (3 oz) light muscovado sugar

25 g (1 oz) pecan nuts or walnuts, chopped or broken into small pieces

2 medium eggs

100 g (4 oz) natural yogurt

3 tablespoons rapeseed oil, plus extra for greasing

1 Preheat the oven to 180°C (fan 160°C/350°F/gas mark 4). Lightly grease a 1 kg (2 lb 4 oz) loaf tin, about 22 x 13 cm (8½ x 5 inches) with rapeseed oil, then line the base with baking parchment. Peel the bananas, break in pieces into a bowl, then mash them as smoothly as you can with a fork – but don't worry if there are a few small lumps. You should have about 200 g (7 oz) banana. Stir in the lemon zest and vanilla.

2 Mix both the flours with the baking powder, bicarbonate of soda and ground almonds in a large mixing bowl. Rub the butter into the flour mixture with your fingertips, then tip in the sugar and rub the mix between your fingers to break down any small lumps of it. Stir in the nuts. Make a well in the centre. Beat the eggs in a bowl, then stir in the yogurt and oil. Tip this mixture along with the mashed banana into the well and briefly and gently stir together with a large metal spoon so that everything is just combined, without overmixing.

3 Spoon the mixture into the tin and level the top. Bake for 50–55 minutes or until a skewer inserted into the centre of the cake comes out clean, laying a piece of foil over the top towards the end if it is starting to brown too quickly. Leave the banana bread in the tin for 5 minutes, then loosen the sides with a round-bladed knife, turn it out on to a wire rack to finish cooling and peel off the lining paper. Keeps moist, well wrapped, for several days.

Reduce the sugar by using dark muscovado for its intense, rich flavour and really ripe bananas – the blacker the better, as they get sweeter and sweeter as they darken

Peanut butter cookies

Just as the name of these cookies conjures up a favourite childhood treat, it's also a giveaway as to the amount of fat and sugar they may contain. By incorporating the familiar ingredients but making a few considered adjustments, this version remains faithful to the original taste and texture while offering a lighter alternative.

	Classic	Lighter
Kcals	149	106
Fat	8.8 g	6.4 g
Sat fat	3.7 g	2 g
Sugar	7.5 g	4.1 g

Per cookie 106 kcals

Protein 2.5g, carbs 9.5g, fat 6.4g, sat fat 2.0g, fibre 0.8g, sugar 4.1g, salt 0.2g

Makes 20

Prep: 25 minutes, plus chilling
Cook: 10–12 minutes

50 g (2 oz) butter, at soft room temperature

50 g (2 oz) light muscovado sugar

25 g (1 oz) golden caster sugar

100 g (4 oz) chunky peanut butter, with no added sugar

1 tablespoon rapeseed oil, plus 2 teaspoons

1 medium egg, beaten

½ teaspoon vanilla extract

140 g (5 oz) plain flour

½ teaspoon baking powder

¼ teaspoon bicarbonate of soda

25 g (1 oz) oven-roasted, unsalted peanuts, roughly chopped

1 Line a large baking sheet with baking parchment (or 2 if you have them). Preheat the oven to 180°C (fan 160°C/350°F/gas mark 4). In a large bowl, beat together the butter, both the sugars and peanut butter with a wooden spoon until light and well blended. Beat in all the oil, then the egg and vanilla extract. Combine the flour, baking powder and bicarbonate of soda, then stir this into the mixture, half at a time, along with the peanuts to make a soft dough. Shape the dough into a log shape, wrap it in baking parchment and chill for 30 minutes.

2 Slice the dough into 20 even-sized pieces, then shape and roll each piece between your hands into small balls. On the work surface, flatten each one with your fingers into a 6 cm (2½ inch) circle, smoothing the tops and neatening the edges. Place them 2.5 cm (1 inch) apart on the lined baking sheet or sheets (bake them in batches if necessary). Press them gently with the back of a fork to make a pattern of lines.

3 Bake for 10–12 minutes or until pale golden. Transfer to a wire rack to cool.

Lower the sugar by using less and enhancing the flavour with vanilla – and choose peanut butter with no added sugar

Chocolate cupcakes

They may be one of the prettiest bakes around, but with the generous swirls of icing on top and buttery sponge below, cupcakes can get incredibly high in fat, saturated fat and sugar. All these, along with calories, have been amazingly reduced – yet these lighter cupcakes have lost none of their irresistible taste and glamour.

	Classic	Lighter
Kcals	459	234
Fat	26.1 g	10.4 g
Sat fat	16 g	4.4 g
Sugar	43.9 g	18.5 g

Per serving 234 kcals

Protein 6.7 g, carbs 27.8 g, fat 10.4 g, sat fat 4.4 g, fibre 1.3 g, sugar 18.5 g, salt 0.6 g

Makes 12

Prep: 35 minutes, plus cooling
Cook: 20 minutes

For the cakes

175 g (6 oz) self-raising flour

2 tablespoons sifted cocoa powder

1½ teaspoons baking powder

140 g (5 oz) golden caster sugar

25 g (1 oz) ground almonds

2 large eggs

175 g (6 oz) natural yogurt

2–3 drops vanilla extract

25 g (1 oz) butter, melted

2 tablespoons rapeseed oil

For the icing

25 g (1 oz) dark chocolate, preferably 70% cocoa solids, finely chopped, plus 1 rounded tablespoon grated chocolate for decorating

25 g (1 oz) butter, at soft room temperature

50 g (2 oz) icing sugar

1 tablespoon cocoa powder

1 teaspoon semi-skimmed milk

100 g (4 oz) light soft cheese, straight from the fridge

100 g (4 oz) quark cheese

Reduce fat as well as sugar by using light soft cheese and quark to give the icing its creamy bulk, instead of using all butter and icing sugar

1 Preheat the oven to 180°C (fan 160°C/350°C/gas mark 4). For the cakes, line a 12-hole muffin tin with pretty paper muffin cases. Tip the flour into a large mixing bowl, remove 2 tablespoons of it and replace with the cocoa. Stir in the baking powder, sugar and ground almonds, then make a well in the centre. Beat the eggs in a separate bowl with a fork and stir in the yogurt and vanilla. Pour this mixture, along with the melted butter and oil, into the dry mixture and stir briefly together with a large metal spoon, just so that everything is well combined.

2 Divide the mixture evenly between the paper cases. Bake for 20 minutes until well risen. Remove and cool completely on a wire rack.

3 To make the icing, tip the chocolate into a heatproof bowl, set it over a pan of gently simmering water (so that the bowl does not touch the water), then remove from the heat and leave until melted and cooled.

4 Put the butter, icing sugar, cocoa and milk in a medium bowl, then beat with a wooden spoon until smooth. Next, beat in the soft cheese and quark. When the chocolate has cooled, stir it into the soft cheese mixture. Spoon, then spread the icing in big swirls over each cupcake and scatter with the grated chocolate. They will keep for up to 2–3 days in the fridge.

Blueberry muffins

These are light, fluffy muffins with added fruit and taste. Adding bananas and lemon will boost the flavour and eliminate the need for salt.

	Classic	Lighter
Kcals	234	206
Fat	9 g	6 g
Sat fat	5 g	1 g
Sugar	16.4 g	16 g

Per muffin 206 kcals

Protein 5 g, carbs 36 g, fat 6 g, sat fat 1 g, fibre 2 g, sugar 16 g, salt 0.43 g

Makes 12

Prep: 25 minutes
Cook: 20–25 minutes

5 tablespoons rapeseed oil

225 g (8 oz) self-raising flour

115 g (4 oz) wholemeal flour

2 teaspoons baking powder

finely grated zest of ½ lemon, plus 1 teaspoon lemon juice

85 g (3 oz) golden caster sugar

50 g (2 oz) light muscovado sugar

1 small very ripe banana with black skin (about 85 g/3 oz peeled weight)

1 large egg

300 ml (½ pint) buttermilk

225 g (8 oz) fresh blueberries

1 Preheat the oven to 200°C (fan 180°C/400°F/gas mark 6). Use 1 teaspoon of the oil to lightly grease a 12-hole muffin tin (or use paper cases).

2 Mix both flours with the baking powder and lemon zest. Reserve 1 tablespoon of the caster sugar, then stir the rest into the flour with the muscovado sugar.

3 Mash the banana well. In another bowl, beat the egg, then stir in the banana, buttermilk and remaining oil. Using a large metal spoon, very lightly stir into the flour mix, just to combine; overmixing will make the muffins tough. Toss in the blueberries and give just a few turns of the spoon to carefully stir them in without crushing.

4 Spoon the mixture into the tin – each hole should be very full. Bake for 20–25 minutes until risen and golden.

5 Mix the reserved caster sugar with the lemon juice. When the muffins are done, remove from the oven, then brush with the sugar and lemon mixture while they are still hot. Gently loosen the edges of each muffin with a knife, then leave in the tin for 15 minutes to cool a little as they are very delicate while hot. Remove to a wire rack. These are best eaten the day of making.

use buttermilk instead of milk to lower fat and saturated fat

Chocolate chip cookies

The size of American cookies seems to get larger and larger, but make them too small and we feel cheated. These cookies are the perfect balancing act of size and ingredients.

	Classic	Lighter
Kcals	162	97
Fat	10 g	5 g
Sat fat	6 g	3 g
Sugar	11 g	6 g

Per cookie 97 kcals

Protein 1 g, carbs 12 g, fat 5 g, sat fat 3 g, fibre 1 g, sugar 6 g, salt 0.12 g

Makes 22

Prep: 25 minutes plus cooling and standing
Cook: 12 minutes per batch

85 g (3 oz) butter

1 tablespoon cocoa powder

1 teaspoon instant coffee granules

85 g (3 oz) light muscovado sugar

25 g (1 oz) golden granulated sugar

85 g (3 oz) dark chocolate, 70% cocoa solids

1 medium egg, beaten

½ teaspoon vanilla extract

140 g (5 oz) plain flour

½ teaspoon bicarbonate of soda

1 Line a couple of baking sheets with baking parchment. Put the butter, cocoa and coffee in a medium saucepan, then heat gently until the butter has melted. Remove from the heat, stir in both the sugars, then leave to cool.

2 Chop the chocolate into small pieces. Beat the egg and vanilla into the cooled butter mix to make a smooth batter. Stir the flour and bicarbonate of soda together. Tip it into the batter mixture with two-thirds of the chocolate, then gently stir together to combine. Don't overmix. Leave for 10–15 minutes to firm up slightly, ready for shaping.

3 Preheat the oven to 180°C (fan 160°C/350°F/gas mark 4). Using your hands, shape the mixture into 22 small balls. Lay them on the lined sheets, spaced well apart so that they have room to spread (you may have to bake in batches). Press the rest of the chocolate pieces on top of each cookie. (They can be frozen on the sheets and then transferred to bags at this stage, and kept in the freezer for up to 1 month.) Bake for 12 minutes. Leave on the sheets for a couple of minutes, then transfer to a wire rack to cool.

Add less sugar, but intensify the flavour and moistness by using granulated mixed with light muscovado

Victoria sandwich

Simply reducing the ingredients won't work with this classic recipe, so I've worked out some alternatives that will still provide the cake's characteristic texture and taste. Now you CAN have your cake and eat it.

	Classic	Lighter
Kcals	371	263
Fat	20.3 g	9.3 g
Sat fat	12 g	2.8 g
Sugar	27.4 g	24.1 g

Per slice 263 kcals

Protein 5.6 g, carbs 39 g, fat 9.3 g, sat fat 2.8 g, fibre 1.3 g, sugar 24.1 g, salt 0.6 g

Cuts into 8 slices

Prep: 25 minutes
Cook: 20 minutes

175 g (6 oz) self-raising flour

1½ teaspoons baking powder

140 g (5 oz) golden caster sugar

25 g (1 oz) ground almonds

2 large eggs

175 g (6 oz) natural yogurt

2–3 drops vanilla extract

25 g (1 oz) butter, melted

2 tablespoons rapeseed oil, plus extra for greasing

4 tablespoons raspberry conserve

½ teaspoon icing sugar, to decorate

1 Preheat the oven to 180°C (fan 160°C/350°F/gas mark 4). Lightly grease 2 x 18 cm (7 inch) sandwich cake tins (preferably loose-bottomed) with rapeseed oil, then line the bases with baking parchment. Tip the flour, baking powder, caster sugar and ground almonds into a large mixing bowl, then make a well in the centre. Beat the eggs in a separate bowl, then stir in the yogurt and vanilla. Pour this mixture, along with the melted butter and oil, into the dry mixture and stir briefly together with a large metal spoon until well combined.

2 Divide the mixture evenly between the 2 tins and level the tops. Bake both cakes, side by side, for 20 minutes until risen and beginning to come away slightly from the edges of the tins.

3 Remove the cakes from the oven and loosen the sides with a round-bladed knife. Let the cakes cool briefly in the tins, then turn them out. If the tins are loose-bottomed, an easy way is to sit the tin on an upturned jam jar and let the outer ring of the tin drop down. Peel off the lining paper and sit the cakes on a wire rack. Leave until completely cold.

4 Put one of the cakes on a serving plate and spread over the conserve. Put the other cake on top and sift over the icing sugar, or make a pattern using a paper template.

Greatly reduce the butter and replace with yogurt and rapeseed oil as substitutes to cut the fat further, especially saturated fat

Flapjacks

Flapjacks hold together in such a mouth-watering way, but that is due to all the butter and sugar required to make the oats stick. The trick in this healthier version is to stir in some grated apple so that less butter and sugar are needed – but each bar remains sticky, chewy and moreish.

	Classic	Lighter
Kcals	215	157
Fat	11.5 g	8.4 g
Sat fat	6.7 g	2.9 g
Sugar	13.1 g	8.3 g

Per flapjack 157 kcals

Protein 3 g, carbs 16.1 g, fat 8.4 g, sat fat 2.9 g, fibre 2.1 g, sugar 8.3 g, salt 0.1 g

Makes 18

Prep: 20 minutes
Cook: 30–35 minutes

85 g (3 oz) butter, cut into pieces

50 g (2 oz) demerara sugar

25 g (1 oz) dark muscovado sugar

3 tablespoons golden syrup

3 tablespoons rapeseed oil

250 g (9 oz) porridge oats (not jumbo)

25 g (1 oz) finely chopped toasted hazelnuts

1 large eating apple, about 250 g (9 oz), peeled and cored

2 tablespoons sunflower seeds

1 tablespoon golden linseed

1 Preheat the oven to 180°C (fan 160°C/350°F/gas mark 4). Line the base of a 28 x 18 cm (11 x 7 inch) shallow baking tin with baking parchment (no need to grease). Put the butter, both sugars and the golden syrup in a medium pan over a medium heat. Heat until the butter has melted, stirring occasionally. The sugar doesn't need to completely dissolve. Remove from the heat and stir in the oil, oats and hazelnuts. Grate the apple on the coarsest side of your grater and stir into the mixture.

2 Tip the oat mixture into the lined tin and spread it out evenly. Scatter over the sunflower seeds and linseeds and pat them firmly into the surface.

3 Bake for 25–30 minutes or until set and golden brown. Loosen the mixture from the sides of the tin so that it doesn't stick. Mark into 18 bars with a sharp knife, then leave to cool before cutting through the markings again and lifting the bars out of the tin.

Reduce fat and sugar by mixing in some grated eating apple to create stickiness and increase fibre

Oat and raisin cookies

Getting the perfect balance of crispness and chewiness for most classic cookies is usually determined by the amount of fat and sugar you need to add. To find ways to get them both to a healthier minimum, I've made careful ingredient and baking choices to ensure that these cookies are still great for munching on.

	Classic	Lighter
Kcals	218	116
Fat	11 g	5.6 g
Sat fat	5.3 g	2 g
Sugar	15.1 g	8.2 g

Per cookie 116 kcals

Protein 1.8 g, carbs 14.2 g, fat 5.6 g, sat fat 2 g, fibre 1 g, sugar 8.2 g, salt 0.1 g

Makes 15

Prep: 25 minutes, plus cooling
Cook: 10 minutes per batch

50 g (2 oz) butter

3 tablespoons rapeseed oil

1 tablespoon golden syrup

50 g (2 oz) plain wholemeal flour

50 g (2 oz) plain flour

50 g (2 oz) porridge oats (not jumbo)

50 g (2 oz) light muscovado sugar

¼ teaspoon baking powder

¼ teaspoon bicarbonate of soda

½ teaspoon ground cinnamon

85 g (3 oz) raisins

1 medium egg, beaten

1 Preheat the oven to 180°C (fan 160°C/350°F/gas mark 4). Line a large baking sheet (or 2 if you have them) with baking parchment.

2 Melt the butter in a small saucepan, then remove from the heat and spoon in the oil and golden syrup. Set aside to cool slightly. Mix both the flours and the oats in a large mixing bowl with the sugar, baking powder, bicarbonate of soda, cinnamon and raisins. Make a well in the centre of the flour mixture, pour in the butter and oil, then add the egg. Stir all together to mix to a soft, slightly sticky dough.

3 Divide, then shape the mixture into 15 smooth, even-sized balls. Place them on the baking sheet, spaced well apart to leave room for the mixture to spread, then flatten with your fingers to about 6 cm (2½ inch) circles. Bake for about 10 minutes (in batches) or until golden. Leave to cool on the baking sheet for a couple of minutes, then transfer to a wire rack to finish cooling.

Line your baking sheet with baking parchment so that you don't need extra butter for greasing

Almond tart

This is my spin on Bakewell tart. The trick is to replace half the almonds with polenta – you cut down on the fat, while maintaining the tart's characeristic texture. The tart is even softer when eaten the next day.

	Classic	Lighter
Kcals	429	280
Fat	28.2 g	16.2 g
Sat fat	12.5 g	3.9 g
Sugar	20.3 g	12.8 g

Per serving 280 kcals

Protein 5.9 g, carbs 27.2 g, fat 16.2 g, sat fat 3.9 g, fibre 1.1 g, sugar 12.8 g, salt 0.4 g

Serves 8

Prep: 25 minutes
Cook: 50 minutes

200 g (7 oz) bought shortcrust pastry

plain flour, for dusting

100 g (4 oz) fresh raspberries

1 tablespoon raspberry conserve or jam

1 tablespoon flaked almonds

1 heaped tablespoon sifted icing sugar

For the filling

50 g (2 oz) ground almonds

50 g (2 oz) polenta

50 g (2 oz) golden caster sugar, plus 2 teaspoons

½ teaspoon baking powder

2 medium eggs

100 g (4 oz) natural yogurt

scant ½ teaspoon almond extract

2 tablespoons rapeseed oil

1 Preheat the oven to 200°C (fan 180°C/400°F/gas mark 6). Thinly roll out the pastry on a lightly floured surface. Line a 20 cm (8 inch) fluted flan tin with the pastry, easing the pastry into the tin carefully to prevent it stretching. Run a rolling pin over the top of the tin to trim off any excess pastry. Prick the pastry base lightly with a fork. Put the tin on a baking sheet. Line the pastry with foil and baking beans and bake for 12 minutes until the pastry is set.

2 Meanwhile, to start the filling, heat a small, dry non-stick pan, tip in the ground almonds and gently heat, stirring often, for 2–3 minutes to lightly brown. Transfer to a mixing bowl to cool.

3 Remove the foil and beans from the pastry case and bake for 5 minutes more until pale golden. Remove and reduce the oven to 180°C (fan 160°C/350°F/gas mark 4).

4 Using a fork, mash the raspberries in a small bowl with the conserve or jam. Spread over the pastry base. Put the polenta, sugar and baking powder in the bowl with the toasted ground almonds and stir to combine. Make a well in the centre. Beat the eggs in a separated bowl, then beat in the yogurt and almond extract. Tip this, along with the oil, into the dry ingredients and gently stir together with a large metal spoon so that everything is just combined – don't overmix.

5 Pour the almond filling over the raspberry mixture and scatter the flaked almonds over the top. Bake for 30 minutes or until the top is risen and pale golden. Cool slightly, then remove from the tin.

6 Mix the icing sugar with a few drops of cold water to make a thickish icing, then use a teaspoon to drizzle it over the cooled tart.

use polenta to replace some of the ground almonds, then enhance the flavour with almond extract

Chocolate log

Though traditionally served at Christmas, this lighter chocolate log, made without butter and cream, can be a year-round favourite. With a few cake-making and ingredient changes, it remains rich and elegant.

	Classic	Lighter
Kcals	482	271
Fat	29 g	13 g
Sat fat	16 g	7 g
Sugar	42 g	22 g

Per serving 271 kcals

Protein 8 g, carbs 33 g, fat 13 g, sat fat 7 g, fibre 1 g, sugar 22 g, salt 0.29 g

Serves 10

Prep: 35 minutes, plus cooling
Cook: 12–15 minutes

For the sponge

rapeseed oil, for greasing

1 teaspoon instant coffee granules

4 large eggs, at room temperature

85 g (3 oz) golden caster sugar, plus extra for rolling

50 g (2 oz) light muscovado sugar

120 g (4½ oz) self-raising flour

2 tablespoons cocoa powder

For the icing

50 g (2 oz) dark chocolate, 70% cocoa solids or more, very finely chopped

250 g (9 oz) light mascarpone cheese

140 g (5 oz) quark cheese

50 g (2 oz) icing sugar

1½ tablespoons cocoa powder

1 teaspoon instant coffee granules

½ teaspoon vanilla extract

holly sprigs, to decorate (optional)

1 Preheat the oven to 190°C (fan 170°C/375°F/gas mark 5). Lightly grease a 23 x 33 cm (9 x 13 inch) Swiss roll tin with rapeseed oil, then line with baking parchment.

2 Mix the coffee for the sponge with 1 tablespoon warm water. Beat the eggs, both sugars and the coffee mix together in a large mixing bowl with an electric whisk for about 8 minutes or until the mixture is thick and airy like meringue and holds a trail when you lift up the beaters.

3 Sift the flour and cocoa powder over the fluffy egg mix, then fold in very gently using a large metal spoon. Pour the mixture evenly into the lined tin and carefully tip it so that it spreads evenly without being deflated. Use a knife if necessary to very gently tease it into the corners. Bake for 12–15 minutes or until the cake feels spongy but firm when touched.

4 Lay a sheet of baking parchment on the work surface and sprinkle with a little caster sugar. Tip the tin upside-down on to the paper and let the cake fall out. Carefully peel off the paper. Roll up the cake lengthways from one of the short ends with the help of the paper, rolling it inside so that the cake doesn't stick. Cool. (The cake becomes even more moist if left overnight wrapped up, then iced the next day.)

5 For the chocolate icing, put the chopped chocolate in a medium heatproof bowl. Heat a small pan of water (one-third full) until boiling, remove it from the heat, then sit the bowl of chocolate over the top. Leave for a few minutes off the heat until melted. Remove the bowl from the pan, then leave the chocolate until it is cool to the touch.

6 Beat the mascarpone and quark together in a mixing bowl, then sift and stir in the icing sugar and cocoa powder. Stir in the cooled melted chocolate (keeping a couple of teaspoons back for drizzling), then the coffee mixed with the vanilla extract.

7 Carefully unroll the cake – don't worry if it cracks a bit – and discard the lining paper. Spread half of the icing over the unrolled cake, then re-roll it, finishing with the join underneath. Place the cake on a serving plate. Swirl the rest of the icing all over the cake to cover it, then drizzle over the reserved melted chocolate. Decorate with sprigs of holly, if you wish.

Replace butter and cream for the icing and filling with light mascarpone and quark to reduce fat

•

use less chocolate and bump up the taste with cocoa, coffee and vanilla extract

•

Make an icing that requires less sugar

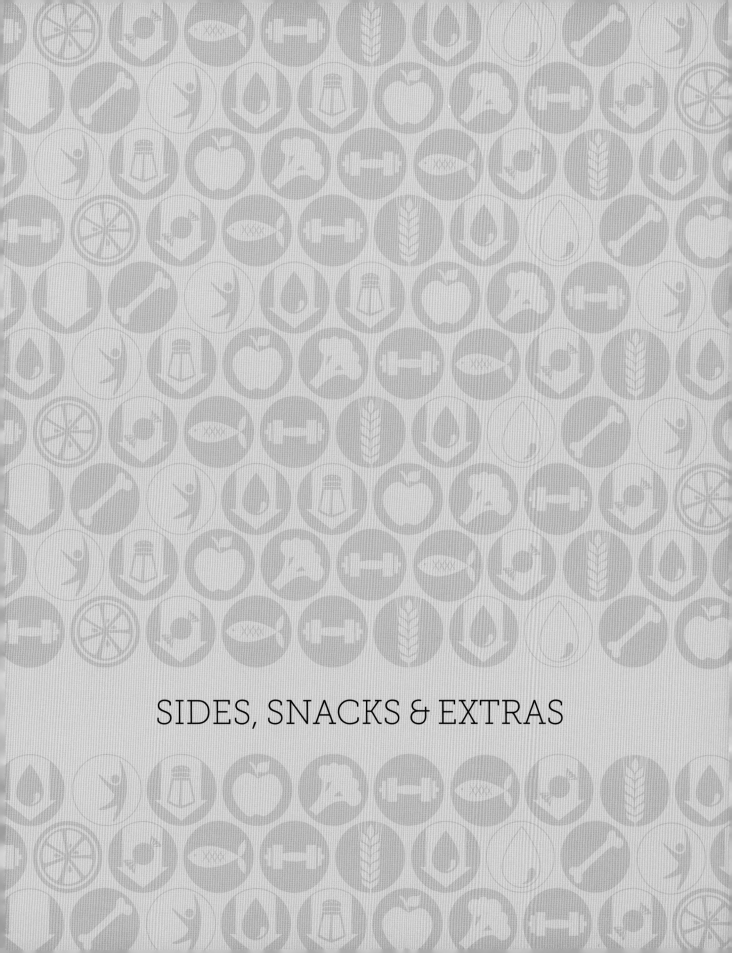

SIDES, SNACKS & EXTRAS

The full English breakfast

Have you ever tucked into a full cooked breakfast, then felt racked with guilt? This is a more contemporary version using sausages with the highest meat content, and as little fat and salt as possible.

	Classic	Lighter
Kcals	807	618
Fat	63 g	37 g
Sat fat	18 g	11 g
Salt	4.52 g	3.05 g

Per serving 618 kcals

Protein 37 g, carbs 37 g, fat 37 g, sat fat 11 g, fibre 5 g, sugar 21 g, salt 3.05 g

Serves 2

Prep: 5 minutes
Cook: about 20 minutes

4 good-quality lean unsmoked back bacon rashers

4 brown-cap portobello mushrooms, trimmed

12–16 cherry tomatoes on the vine, at room temperature

6 teaspoons olive oil

2 slices granary or wholegrain bread, cut on the diagonal

2 good-quality pork sausages, minimum 86% pork

2 large eggs, at room temperature

few drops cider vinegar

2 x 100 ml (3½ fl oz) glasses freshly squeezed orange juice

1 orange, cut into wedges

handful of fresh blueberries, about 50 g (2 oz) total weight

1 Lay the bacon, mushrooms and tomatoes on a foil-lined baking sheet. Brush the tops of the mushrooms with 3 teaspoons of the oil and both sides of the bread with the remaining oil. Set aside.

2 Preheat the grill to high. Lay the sausages on a small foil-lined baking sheet (best not to prick good-quality sausages or they may lose moisture). Grill for about 10 minutes until cooked, turning occasionally.

3 Meanwhile, three-quarters fill a small pan and a wide, deep sauté pan with water. Bring both to the boil. Lower one whole egg into the small pan and remove after 30 seconds. Crack the egg into a cup. Add vinegar to the larger pan, then, using a wire whisk, swirl the water around to create a whirlpool. Remove the whisk and slowly tip the egg into the centre of the whirlpool. When the water comes back to the boil, remove the pan from the heat, cover and leave for 3 minutes, then remove the egg. Place in a bowl of warm water while you cook the other egg. Alternatively, cook both eggs an hour ahead, leave in a bowl of iced water, then reheat for 1½ minutes in simmering water before serving.

4 While the eggs are cooking, heat a griddle pan to very hot. Place the bacon, tomatoes, mushrooms and tomatoes under the grill for 3–4 minutes without turning. At the same time, lay the bread on the griddle pan and cook for about 1 minute each side until crisp. Drain everything on kitchen paper.

5 Remove the eggs with a slotted spoon and drain briefly on kitchen paper. Arrange everything on a plate and serve with the juice and fruit.

choose ingredients wisely by checking and comparing amounts on the labels of bread, bacon and sausages to reduce salt

Crunchy granola

Many granolas are overly sweet, and with all the seeds, nuts and oil to make them crunchy, are in danger of being too high in fat. This one still packs a good crunch and will keep you going all through the morning.

	Classic	Lighter
Kcals	283	236
Fat	17.6 g	13.2 g
Sat fat	2.1 g	1.5 g
Sugar	7.6 g	4.4 g

Per serving 236 kcals

Protein 7.1 g, carbs 19.5 g, fat 13.2 g, sat fat 1.5 g, fibre 4.5 g, sugar 4.4 g, salt 0 g

Makes 18 x 50 g (2 oz) servings

Prep: 15 minutes
Cook: 20–25 minutes

450 g (1 lb) porridge oats (not jumbo)

25 g (1 oz) whole almonds, in skins, sliced or chopped

50 g (2 oz) pecan nuts, chopped

50 g (2 oz) hazelnuts, in skins, roughly chopped

50 g (2 oz) sunflower seeds

50 g (2 oz) pumpkin seeds

4 tablespoons golden linseeds

3 tablespoons sesame seeds

4 tablespoons rapeseed oil

2 tablespoons clear honey

2 teaspoons black treacle

50 g (2 oz) dried blueberries or cranberries

1 Preheat the oven to 190°C (fan 170°C/375°F/gas mark 5). Line a large baking sheet with baking parchment. Tip the oats into a large bowl, then stir in all the nuts and seeds.

2 Measure the rapeseed oil into a small bowl and stir in the honey and black treacle. Pour this into the bowl of oats and give it all a good stir so that everything is evenly coated and to break up any clumps of oats that form. I find a large fork does this job best.

3 Spread the mix on to the baking sheet. The mixture needs to spread out so that it can brown in the oven. Bake for 20–25 minutes, forking through 2–3 times so that the bits underneath that aren't getting brown can come to the surface. When golden all through, remove from the oven and stir in the dried blueberries or cranberries. Leave to cool and become crunchy, then pack into an airtight container to store.

TIPS

• If you measure the oil first in the measuring spoon, then pour the honey into it afterwards without washing it, the honey just slides out.

• Stir the dried fruit in after baking rather than before, otherwise cooking hardens it.

use a little black treacle to help sweeten. its concentrated taste means you need less honey or added sugar

Spanish omelette

Traditionally, the sliced potatoes and onions for a Spanish omelette are stewed in a copious amount of oil before being stirred into the eggs. To lighten up the recipe, I've cooked them in the oven instead.

	Classic	Lighter
Kcals	558	295
Fat	38.9 g	16.5 g
Sat fat	6.7 g	3.5 g
Salt	0.6 g	0.5 g

Per serving 295 kcals

Protein 12.1 g, carbs 24.2 g, fat 16.5 g, sat fat 3.5 g, fibre 4.2 g, sugar 6.3 g, salt 0.5 g

Serves 4

Prep: 25 minutes
Cook: 35 minutes

1 medium onion, very thinly sliced

1 red pepper, cored, deseeded and thinly sliced

3 tablespoons extra virgin olive oil

500 g (1 lb 2 oz) new potatoes, unpeeled and thinly sliced

100 g (4 oz) spinach leaves

6 medium eggs

4 tablespoons chopped flat leaf parsley

salt and freshly ground black pepper

1 Preheat the oven to 190°C (fan 170°C/375°F/gas mark 5). Scatter the onion on one half of a small, non-stick baking sheet and the pepper slices on the other half. Drizzle 1 teaspoon of the oil over the onion slices and another teaspoon over the pepper. Gently toss to coat, keeping them separate, and spread out. Scatter the potatoes over a large, non-stick baking sheet and drizzle over 1 tablespoon of the oil. Toss together and season all the vegetables with black pepper. Roast for 20–25 minutes until softened and tender but not too brown.

2 Put the spinach in a heatproof bowl and pour over enough almost boiling water to let it wilt. Leave for 30 seconds, stir, then tip it into a colander and cool under cold running water. Squeeze out all the liquid, then finely chop.

3 Beat the eggs with a fork in a large mixing bowl and pour in the cold water. Tip in the onion, potatoes, pepper, spinach and 3 tablespoons of the parsley, and season with more pepper and a little salt. Let the mixture stand for about 5 minutes to combine the flavours.

4 Pour 1 tablespoon of the oil into a 23–25 cm (9–10 inch) non-stick frying pan and heat over a medium heat. Stir the egg mixture, pour it into the pan and spread it out evenly. As it starts to set, tip the pan to pour some of the runny egg to the edges. After 6–7 minutes when the edges are cooked, the underneath is slightly browned and the inside not quite cooked, check that the omelette is not sticking on the bottom, then carefully invert it on to a large plate.

5 Pour the remaining 1 teaspoon oil into the pan, then slide the omelette and any runny egg back in. Tuck the edges under to shape the omelette like a plump cushion and cook for about 4 more minutes until just set. Remove and let it stand and settle for 3–4 minutes before serving. Serve hot, warm or cold, scattered with the remaining parsley.

Lower the fat by roasting the vegetables in the oven with minimum oil, then cooking the omelette in a non-stick pan

Roast vegetables

Roasted vegetables can always tempt with their golden crispiness, but this requires generous amounts of oil for cooking. In this recipe, oil is kept to a minimum by cooking the vegetables the French way, en papillote, snugly wrapped in baking parchment, so that all the flavour is trapped inside as they roast, yet they still turn deliciously golden and crisp.

	Classic	Lighter
Kcals	198	141
Fat	8.9 g	3.8 g
Sat fat	1.3 g	0.4 g
Salt	0.3 g	0.2 g

Per serving 141 kcals

Protein 4 g, carbs 22.2 g, fat 3.8 g, sat fat 0.4 g, fibre 3.7 g, sugar 5.4 g, salt 0.2 g

Serves 4

Prep: 15 minutes
Cook: 30 minutes

1 red pepper

1 medium courgette

400 g (14 oz) new potatoes, unpeeled, scrubbed and halved

4 small shallots, halved

8 garlic cloves, peeled

4 sprigs of rosemary

4 teaspoons rapeseed oil

salt and freshly ground black pepper

1 Preheat the oven to 200°C (fan 180°C/400°F/gas mark 6). Cut out 4 x 38 cm (15 inch) squares of baking parchment.

2 Quarter and remove the core and seeds from the pepper, then cut each quarter into 4 to give you 16 pieces. Cut the courgette into 12 thick slices.

3 Lay a quarter of all the vegetables in the centre of each paper square along with 2 garlic cloves and a sprig of rosemary. Drizzle 1 teaspoon of the oil over each one. Season with pepper and a pinch of salt. Fold the edges of the paper over to make a well-sealed parcel.

4 Place the parcels on a large baking sheet and roast for 30 minutes until the vegetables are tender and golden.

TIPS

- Cut the vegetables into similar-sized pieces, so that they all cook evenly together.
- This mixture of vegetables makes a good accompaniment to roast chicken or fish.

Halve the fat by roasting in paper parcels and keep saturated fat to a minimum with rapeseed oil

Hummus

One thing people love about hummus is its soft creamy texture, which comes from blending chickpeas until smooth with tahini and olive oil. By mixing in yogurt and roasted garlic I discovered it's not necessary to use as much tahini and oil, as this lighter recipe still tastes surprisingly rich and creamy, and fat and saturated fat are more than halved.

	Classic	Lighter
Kcals	233	145
Fat	18.9 g	8.2 g
Sat fat	2.6 g	1 g
Salt	0.4 g	0.5 g

Per serving 145 kcals

Protein 6.8 g, carbs 11.4 g, fat 8.2 g, sat fat 1 g, fibre 4.5 g, sugar 1.1 g, salt 0.5 g

Serves 4

Prep: 15 minutes
Cook: 25–30 minutes

1 whole garlic bulb

1 teaspoon cumin seeds

400 g (14 oz) can chickpeas

2 tablespoons lemon juice, plus extra to taste (optional)

1½ tablespoons tahini

1 tablespoon rapeseed oil

2 tablespoons natural yogurt

salt

pinch of paprika and chopped flat leaf parsley, to garnish

1 Preheat the oven to 190°C (fan 170°C/375°F/gas mark 5). Slice the stem end from the garlic to slightly expose the tops of the cloves. Sit the bulb in a small baking tin, then roast for 25–30 minutes until the cloves feel soft.

2 Meanwhile, heat a small, heavy-based pan, tip in the cumin seeds and heat for about a minute or until they start to smell fragrant and darken slightly in colour, moving them around in the pan so that they don't burn. Grind them finely using a pestle and mortar.

3 Drain the chickpeas in a sieve over a bowl. Tip the chickpeas into a blender or food processor with the lemon juice and 3 tablespoons cold water. When the garlic is softened, remove, and when cool enough to handle, separate the cloves from the bulb, squeeze out the soft flesh and put it in with the chickpeas. Process until smooth, then spoon in the tahini, 1 teaspoon of the oil, the yogurt, ½ teaspoon of the toasted cumin and a pinch of salt. Pulse again until soft and creamy.

4 Taste to see if you would like more lemon juice. Also, if you prefer an even softer texture, add a drop more water. Spoon and spread the hummus on to 1 large or 2 small plates using the back of a spoon to give it a swirl. Scatter over a pinch of paprika, chopped parsley and as much of the remaining cumin as you wish, then finish with a drizzle of the remaining oil.

Reduce fat by replacing some of the oil and tahini with yogurt, water and roasted garlic to maintain flavour and creaminess

Sausage rolls

You can send the calories packing with this healthier version of a picnic favourite. It is not always clear what goes into cheaper sausagemeats, so here I've used lean pork mince, which is lower in fat.

	Classic	Lighter
Kcals	178	99
Fat	13.8 g	5.5 g
Sat fat	5 g	2 g
Salt	0.83 g	0.27 g

Per sausage roll 99 kcals

Protein 5.9 g, carbs 6.8 g, fat 5.5 g, sat fat 2 g, fibre 0.6 g, sugar 0.3 g, salt 0.27 g

Makes 16

Prep: 25 minutes, plus cooling and optional chilling
Cook: 20 minutes

For the filling

1 teaspoon rapeseed oil

1 plump shallot, finely chopped

100 g (4 oz) green lentils (drained weight from a 400 g/14 oz can)

300 g (11 oz) 8% fat pork mince

50 g (2 oz) fresh white breadcrumbs

2 teaspoons finely chopped tarragon

good pinch of English mustard powder

good pinch of grated nutmeg

plain flour, for dusting

For the pastry

½ x 375 g (13 oz) sheet ready-rolled puff pastry

2 teaspoons semi-skimmed milk, to glaze

salt and freshly ground black pepper

1 Preheat the oven to 220°C (fan 200°C/425°F/gas mark 7). Line a baking sheet with baking parchment.

2 Heat the oil in a small, non-stick frying pan. Tip in the shallot and fry for a few minutes until softened. Leave to cool. Meanwhile, mash the lentils in a bowl with the back of a spoon, then stir in the rest of the filling ingredients, the shallot, a small pinch of salt and a good grating of black pepper. Cover and chill for 20 minutes (not essential but makes it easier to shape).

3 Halve the filling. Lightly flour the work surface and, using your hands, roll each half, one at a time, into a 28 cm (11 inch) long sausage shape – dust more flour on the work surface if it starts to stick. Set aside.

4 Roll out the pastry on a lightly floured work surface to a 28 cm (11 inch) square. Cut in half to give 2 rectangles. Lay one of the sausage shapes along one of the long edges of one pastry rectangle. Roll the pastry around it to almost enclose, then brush a little milk down the opposite long side. Roll the join underneath and press down to seal. Trim off the ends to neaten if necessary, then slice into 8 rolls. Place on a baking sheet, with the joins underneath. Using the blunt side of the knife, make 3 indents on top of each roll. Repeat with the rest of the pastry and filling. Brush the tops with a little milk.

5 Bake for 18–20 minutes until golden and slightly puffy. Remove from the sheet and cool on a wire rack. Serve warm or cold.

use lean pork mince instead of sausagemeat to reduce the fat. substitute some of the meat with green lentils to reduce saturated fat

Cornish pasties

Don't miss out on a lunchtime favourite. The key to this healthier recipe is in the pastry – how it's made, decreasing the size of the traditionally large pasty and reducing the thickness of the crust.

	Classic	Lighter
Kcals	821	511
Fat	50.6 g	25.2 g
Sat fat	27.8 g	10.7 g
Salt	1.9 g	0.8 g

Per pasty 511 kcals

Protein 22.1 g, carbs 48.5 g, fat 25.2 g, sat fat 10.7 g, fibre 2.8 g, sugar 3.1 g, salt 0.8 g

Makes 6

Prep: 1 hour
Cook: 50 minutes

For the filling

400 g (14 oz) beef skirt, trimmed of excess fat, cut into small chunks

140 g (5 oz) potato, diced

140 g (5 oz) swede, diced

100 g (4 oz) onion, finely chopped

3 tablespoons chopped parsley

1 tablespoon Worcestershire sauce

For the pastry

350 g (12 oz) plain flour, plus extra for dusting

1¼ teaspoons baking powder

85 g (3 oz) cold butter, cut into small pieces

3 tablespoons extra virgin rapeseed oil

1 large egg, separated

salt and freshly ground black pepper

1 Preheat the oven to 200°C (fan 180°C/400°F/gas mark 6). Line 1–2 baking sheets with baking parchment.

2 To make the filling, mix everything together in a bowl with ¾ teaspoon black pepper and 1 tablespoon cold water. Stir in a pinch of salt and set aside.

3 To make the pastry, put the flour, baking powder and butter in a food processor. Pulse until the mixture resembles fine breadcrumbs. Tip in the oil, egg yolk and 5 tablespoons cold water. Pulse again until the dough just starts to come together, adding another ½–1 tablespoon water, or as needed. If you gently press the dough and it sticks together, you know that it's the right consistency. Tip out the dough on to the work surface and gently press it into a smooth ball.

4 Cut the pastry into 6 equal pieces. For each pasty, lightly and briefly shape one piece of the pastry into a smooth ball. (Keep the other pieces wrapped in clingfilm until needed.) Press the ball down to make an even flattened round. Then roll the pastry out on a lightly floured surface, as thinly as you can, to a circle just over 20 cm (8 inches) in diameter. As you are rolling the pastry thinner than usual, handle it carefully to prevent it breaking, and keep the work surface and rolling pin lightly dusted with flour to prevent the pastry sticking. Use the base of a 20 cm (8 inch) loose-bottomed cake tin (or similar) as a guide to cut around to neaten the pastry edges.

5 Spoon a sixth of the filling down the centre of the pastry circle and lightly press down with your hand to contain and flatten it slightly. Dampen the pastry edges with water and carefully bring one side of the pastry over to join the other side, tucking in the filling to keep it inside as you do so. Press the joins together to seal, then make a thin decorative edge by rolling or curling the pastry edge over all the way around. Press down to seal. Repeat with the remaining pastry and filling.

6 Sit each pasty on the lined baking sheet(s), then pierce a small hole in the top of each one for the steam to escape. Beat the egg white to loosen, then brush a little over each pasty to glaze.

7 Bake for 15 minutes, then reduce the oven temperature to 180°C (fan 160°C/350°F/gas mark 4). Brush with more egg white, and bake for a further 35 minutes until the pastry is crisp and golden, covering loosely with foil if they are browning too quickly. Remove with a wide spatula and leave to cool slightly on a wire rack. Serve warm or cold.

Lower fat by trimming any excess from the meat

•

use less fat in the pastry, replacing some of the butter with rapeseed oil to reduce the level of saturated fat

•

Roll the pastry out thinner so that less is required

•

season the filling generously with pepper so that less salt is needed

Garlic bread

Oozing with butter as you take the first mouthful, garlic bread is a treat that can set your heart pounding just thinking of it. With a few sneaky changes, this recipe has half the saturated fat of the classic, but its rich garlicky taste still soaks deeply into each slice of bread.

	Classic	Lighter
Kcals	230	160
Fat	11.4 g	8.3 g
Sat fat	6.7 g	3.1 g
Salt	0.8 g	0.6 g

Per serving (2 slices) 160 kcals

Protein 4.8 g, carbs 16.6 g, fat 8.3 g, sat fat 3.1 g, fibre 1.3 g, sugar 1.1 g, salt 0.6 g

Serves 8 (2 slices per serving)

Prep: 20 minutes
Cook: 12 minutes

25 g (1 oz) unsalted butter, at room temperature

25 g (1 oz) mayonnaise

50 g (2 oz) mozzarella cheese, grated

2 teaspoons extra virgin olive oil

3 garlic cloves, crushed

1 tablespoon finely chopped parsley

1 tablespoon snipped chives

270 g (9½ oz) ciabatta loaf

freshly ground black pepper

1 Preheat the oven to 190°C (fan 170°C/375°F/gas mark 5). Beat the butter and mayonnaise together in a bowl until well blended and smooth. Mix in the mozzarella, oil and garlic, then stir in the parsley and chives. Season with a little pepper.

2 Slice the ciabatta in half horizontally. Spread the garlic mixture over the cut sides of each half. Wrap each half loosely in foil. Place both parcels on a large baking sheet and bake for 10 minutes. Remove.

3 Preheat the grill to high. Open up the parcels and grill for about 2 minutes or until bubbling, crisp and golden. Slice each piece into 8 to serve.

Halve the saturated fat by replacing most of the butter with a mixture of mozzarella cheese, mayonnaise and olive oil

Braised leeks and peas

It's low in fat, counts as one of your five a day, is good for you and packed full of flavours. Serve this as a side dish with salmon or chicken.

	Classic	Lighter
Kcals	90	56
Fat	4.1 g	1.9 g
Sat fat	2.3 g	0.3 g
Salt	0.2 g	0.4 g

Per serving 56 kcals

Protein 3.6 g, carbs 6.1 g, fat 1.9 g, sat fat 0.3 g, fibre 3.5 g, sugar 2.5 g, salt 0.4 g

Serves 6

Prep: 5 minutes
Cook: 20 minutes

6 leeks, trimmed

250 ml (9 fl oz) chicken or vegetable stock

3 garlic cloves, sliced

4 sprigs of thyme, plus extra leaves to serve

200 g (7oz) frozen peas

2 teaspoons olive oil

freshly ground black pepper

1 Discard the outer, darker, tougher leaves from the leeks, then halve each into 2 shorter lengths and rinse under cold running water.

2 Pour the chicken or vegetable stock into a large, wide shallow pan, then scatter in the garlic and sprigs of thyme. Lay the leeks in the pan, trying not to crowd them, then season with pepper. Cover and simmer for 15 minutes until almost tender.

3 Add the peas to the pan, bring back to the boil and simmer for a further 5 minutes until the vegetables are cooked.

4 Using a slotted spoon, transfer the leeks, peas and garlic to a warm serving dish, season with extra pepper, drizzle over the olive oil and finish with a scattering of thyme leaves.

Replace butter with olive oil to lower saturated fat. and create extra flavour with garlic and thyme

Ratatouille

By roasting the aubergines with the other vegetables instead of frying them, the fat is kept to a minimum. To enhance the flavour I've borrowed food writer Elizabeth David's idea of adding crushed coriander seeds.

	Classic	Lighter
Kcals	249	161
Fat	18.2 g	8.8 g
Sat fat	2.8 g	1.4 g
Salt	0.9 g	0.2 g

Per serving 161 kcals

Protein 5.1 g, carbs 15.6 g, fat 8.8 g, sat fat 1.4 g, fibre 7.5 g, sugar 13.7 g, salt 0.2 g

Serves 4

Prep: 35 minutes
Cook: 45 minutes

2 red peppers, cored, deseeded and cut into 2.5 cm (1 inch) pieces

2 medium courgettes, cut into 2.5 cm (1 inch) pieces

1 large aubergine, cut into 2.5 cm (1 inch) pieces

2 tablespoons olive oil, plus 2 teaspoons

2 sprigs of thyme

2 sprigs of rosemary

1 bay leaf

1 onion, chopped

4 garlic cloves, finely chopped

450 g (1 lb) tomatoes

1 teaspoon coriander seeds, crushed

salt and freshly ground black pepper

handful of chopped fresh coriander and flat leaf parsley, to garnish

1 Preheat the oven to 200°C (fan 180°C/ 400°F/gas mark 6). Scatter the peppers, then the courgettes and aubergine on to a large, shallow roasting tray or baking sheet, keeping them all separate. Drizzle the aubergine with 1 tablespoon of the oil and the peppers and courgettes with one more tablespoon between them. Toss well so that they are all coated in the oil, still keeping them separate and in a single layer, then season with pepper and a little salt. Roast for 30–35 minutes or until softened and tinged brown.

2 Meanwhile, make a tomato sauce. Wrap the thyme and rosemary in the bay leaf to make a bouquet garni and tie up with plain string. Heat the 2 teaspoons oil in a large saucepan or sauté pan. Tip in the onion and garlic and fry on a medium-low heat for about 10 minutes until softened but not browned, stirring occasionally. Halve the tomatoes, cut out their cores, then roughly chop. Stir the tomatoes and the bouquet garni in with the onion and cook, still on a lowish heat, for about 20–25 minutes or until of a sauce consistency.

3 Tip the roasted vegetables into the tomato sauce, scraping the juices in too. Stir in the crushed coriander, then cover and warm through briefly to bring everything together, but still keeping the shape of the vegetables. Remove the bouquet garni, season with more pepper if needed and scatter over the chopped coriander and parsley to serve.

TIP

- Although usually served as a warm or hot vegetable accompaniment, ratatouille is also good served at room temperature as a light lunch or supper. Though it will up the fat slightly, a little crumbled feta cheese scattered over the top makes it quite substantial.

Flavour with coriander seeds and you won't need much salt

Creamed garlicky spinach

Toss spinach in a creamy sauce and you have a very special vegetable side dish, but with butter and cream used to enrich the sauce, fat levels can be high. I've come up with a flavoursome, creamy sauce that needs neither of those ingredients, and calories and fats are more than halved.

	Classic	Lighter
Kcals	192	83
Fat	12.9 g	3.1 g
Sat fat	7.7 g	1.6 g
Salt	0.8 g	0.6 g

Per serving 83 kcals

Protein 5.5 g, carbs 8.3 g, fat 3.1 g, sat fat 1.6 g, fibre 3.1 g, sugar 4.8 g, salt 0.6 g

Serves 4

Prep: 15 minutes
Cook: 15 minutes

1 tablespoon cornflour

250 ml (9 fl oz) semi-skimmed milk

2 garlic cloves, finely chopped

1 large or 2 small shallots, very finely chopped

400 g (14 oz) spinach leaves

good pinch of grated nutmeg, plus extra to garnish

2 tablespoons half-fat crème fraîche

salt and freshly ground black pepper

1 Mix the cornflour with 1 tablespoon of the milk in a small bowl and set aside. Pour the rest of the milk into a medium saucepan. Drop in the chopped garlic and shallot, bring just to the boil, then lower the heat and simmer very gently for 6–8 minutes to soften them. Set aside to infuse.

2 Meanwhile, put the spinach in a large, heatproof bowl and pour over water straight from the kettle that is almost boiling. Leave for 30–45 seconds to wilt, turning it in the water as it sits. Drain off the water and tip the spinach into a colander. Leave for a minute or two to finish off wilting, turning it over occasionally, then, when cool enough to handle (if it's not, refresh it quickly under cold running water and drain), squeeze out any excess water really well with the back of a wooden spoon or your hands. Chop the spinach.

3 Re-stir the cornflour mix, then stir it into the infused milk. Put the pan on the heat and bring to the boil, stirring until thickened and smooth. Remove from the heat, then season with pepper, a small pinch of salt and the nutmeg. Stir in the crème fraîche.

4 Stir the spinach into the sauce and warm through briefly on a low heat. If heated for too long, the spinach will lose its vibrant colour. Serve sprinkled with an extra pinch of nutmeg to garnish.

Reduce fat by making a butter-less sauce with cornflour and milk, infused with shallot and garlic to boost the taste

Potato Dauphinoise

Potato Dauphinoise relies on butter, milk and cream for its extravagant richness. What makes this dish hard to adapt is that the recipe also relies on the potatoes cooking in, and marrying with, these ingredients to create a creamy sauce, but I've made this lighter version just as special.

	Classic	Lighter
Kcals	424	232
Fat	32.3 g	12 g
Sat fat	18.4 g'	7 g
Salt	0.82 g	0.25 g

Per serving 232 kcals

Protein 6 g, carbs 27 g, fat 12 g, sat fat 7 g, fibre 2 g, sugar 3 g, salt 0.25 g

Serves 6

Prep: 30 minutes, plus infusing
Cook: about 1½ hours

1 teaspoon olive oil

150 ml (¼ pint) semi-skimmed milk

1 plump garlic clove, peeled and halved

4 sprigs of thyme, plus extra small sprigs for sprinkling

1 bay leaf

1 shallot, roughly chopped

good pinch of freshly grated nutmeg

1 kg (2 lb 4 oz) waxy potatoes, such as Desirée

140 g (5 oz) full-fat crème fraîche

75 ml (2½ fl oz) vegetable stock

1 teaspoon thyme leaves

25 g (1 oz) Gruyère cheese or vegetarian alternative, grated

salt and freshly ground black pepper

1 Preheat the oven to 160°C (fan 140°C/325°F/gas mark 3). Brush the oil over the bottom and sides of a 25 x 18 x 5 cm (10 x 7 x 2 inch) ovenproof dish. Put the milk, garlic, the 4 sprigs of thyme, bay leaf and shallot into a saucepan. Bring just to the boil, then remove from the heat and add the nutmeg and a little pepper. Set aside to infuse while you prepare the potatoes.

2 Peel, then slice the potatoes very thinly. Pat them dry. Layer half of the slices in the dish, overlapping slightly, then season with pepper and a little salt.

3 Strain the infused milk into a jug. Put the crème fraîche into a bowl, then gradually pour in the milk, whisking until smooth. Add the stock and thyme leaves. Return this liquid to the jug, then pour half of it over the potatoes in the dish.

4 Layer the rest of the potatoes in the dish, then add the remaining liquid, the cheese and a grind of pepper. Sit the dish on a baking sheet and bake for 1¼–1½ hours until golden and tender – test by inserting a sharp knife through the potatoes. Let it stand for 5 minutes before serving, sprinkled with small sprigs of thyme.

Lower fat by eliminating cream and butter. Use crème fraîche combined with stock and semi-skimmed milk instead

Pesto

There are many versions of this fragrantly flavoured Italian sauce, but most require lots of oil, high-fat pine nuts and Parmesan. It wouldn't be a classic pesto without them though, so by introducing fewer high-fat ingredients to complement and bulk out the traditional ones, saturated fat is greatly reduced but it still tastes like the real thing.

	Classic	Lighter
Kcals	91	56
Fat	9.1 g	5.6 g
Sat fat	1.7 g	0.8 g
Salt	0.1 g	0.1 g

Per tablespoon 56 kcals

Protein 1.2 g, carbs 0.3 g, fat 5.6 g, sat fat 0.8 g, fibre 0.3 g, sugar 0.2 g, salt 0.1 g

Makes 300 ml (½ pint)

Prep: 10 minutes
Cook: 5 minutes

25 g (1 oz) pine nuts

85 g (3 oz) tenderstem broccoli spears

25 g (1 oz) basil

25 g (1 oz) Parmesan cheese, finely diced

2 garlic cloves, roughly chopped

3 tablespoons olive oil

2 tablespoons rapeseed oil, plus 1 teaspoon

salt and freshly ground black pepper

1 Toast the pine nuts in a small, heavy-based pan over a medium heat until golden, moving them around in the pan often so that they brown evenly. Set aside.

2 Chop the broccoli spears very finely and put them in a small pan of boiling water to blanch. Bring back to the boil, then cook for 2 minutes so that the broccoli still has a bit of bite and keeps its colour. Immediately drain the broccoli in a sieve and put under cold running water to stop it cooking and keep its freshness. Drain well.

3 Strip the leaves from the basil stems and put them in the food processor with the pine nuts, Parmesan and garlic. Pulse briefly to combine and roughly chop. Tip in the broccoli, and with the machine running, pour in the olive oil and the tablespoons rapeseed oil. Don't over-process the mixture, as you want to keep some texture. Season with a little pepper and a pinch of salt.

4 Transfer to a bowl and pour over the extra 1 teaspoon rapeseed oil to protect the surface. It will keep in the fridge for 3–4 days. It also freezes well.

Toast the pine nuts to heighten their flavour, then use fewer to reduce fat further and let tenderstem broccoli spears provide any loss of bulk

Red onion marmalade

As with any preserve, sugar is bound to be high, and as the onions are traditionally fried to caramelize them, fat can be high too. To bring the sugar levels down by nearly half, I've found other ways to sweeten this marmalade, and to reduce the fat, I've completely changed the way it is cooked, yet the taste is still great and the texture irresistibly sticky.

	Classic	Lighter
Kcals	27	14
Fat	1.2 g	0.4 g
Sat fat	0.3 g	0 g
Sugar	3.2 g	1.8 g
Salt	0.1 g	0g

Per tablespoon 14 kcals

Protein 0.3 g, carbs 2.2 g, fat 0.4 g, sat fat 0g, fibre 0.4 g, sugar 1.8 g, salt 0g

Makes 550 ml (19 fl oz)

Prep: 25 minutes
Cook: about 1 hour

950 g (2 lb 2 oz) red onions, peeled

3 garlic cloves, chopped

1½ teaspoons mustard seeds

2 sprigs of thyme

¼ teaspoon salt

1½ tablespoons rapeseed oil

25 g (1 oz) light muscovado sugar

2 teaspoons black treacle

50 ml (1 fl oz) dry white wine

2 tablespoons red wine vinegar

1 tablespoon balsamic vinegar

freshly ground black pepper

1 Preheat the oven to 190°C (fan 170°C/375°F/gas mark 5). Halve the onions lengthways, then slice very thinly with the cut side facing down. Put the onions, garlic, mustard seeds and thyme sprigs in a large roasting tin. Sprinkle over the salt and a good grinding of pepper. Pour over the oil and toss together with your hands to coat well. Spread the onions out in a single layer and roast for about 40 minutes, stirring twice, until well reduced and softened. Increase the oven temperature to 200°C (fan 180°C/400°F/gas mark 6) and roast for a further 15–20 minutes until the onions are starting to stick and caramelize on the bottom of the pan.

2 Remove from the oven, discard the thyme sprigs and stir in the sugar, treacle, wine and both vinegars. Transfer the onion mixture and any juices to a medium saucepan. Rinse the roasting tin out with 75 ml (2½ fl oz) water and stir these juices into the onions in the saucepan. Bring the mixture up to a gentle bubble and let it cook for about 5 minutes or until the juices get a little bit sticky.

3 Spoon the onion marmalade into small, clean, sterilized lidded glass jars. It will keep for at least a month in a cool, dry place.

Choose red onions for their natural sweet flavour so that added sugar can be reduced and calories lowered

Scotch eggs

This lighter version of Scotch eggs involves substituting some of the pork mince with lentils and shallow-frying the eggs before baking in the oven. These are at their best eaten the day they are made.

	Classic	Lighter
Kcals	529	223
Fat	42.6 g	11.7 g
Sat fat	9.3 g	2.6 g
Salt	2 g	0.5 g

Per Scotch egg 223 kcals

Protein 21 g, carbs 8.3 g, fat 11.7 g, sat fat 2.6 g, fibre 1.4 g, sugar 0.3 g, salt 0.5 g

Makes 4

Prep: 40 minutes, plus cooling and chilling
Cook: 25 minutes

5 teaspoons rapeseed oil

1 shallot, finely chopped

5 medium eggs

85 g (3 oz) green lentils (drained weight from a 400 g/14 oz can)

225 g (8 oz) less than 5% fat mince pork

2 teaspoons finely chopped sage

3 teaspoons finely snipped chives

½ teaspoon English mustard powder

good pinch of grated nutmeg

1 tablespoon plain flour

25 g (1 oz) Japanese panko breadcrumbs

salt and freshly ground black pepper

1 Heat 1 teaspoon of the oil in a small, non-stick frying pan. Tip in the shallot and fry for a few minutes until softened. Transfer to a plate and set aside to cool. (No need to wash the pan, as you can use it later.)

2 Meanwhile, put 4 of the eggs in a medium pan, covering well with cold water. Bring to the boil – as the water starts to bubble, set the timer and boil for 5 minutes. When cooked, pour off the boiling water and cool the eggs under cold running water to stop them from cooking further.

3 Mash the lentils well in a medium bowl with the back of a fork, then stir in the pork mince, sage, 2 teaspoons of the chives, the mustard powder, nutmeg, cooled shallots, a pinch of salt and a generous grating of black pepper. Peel the shells from the eggs and pat dry with kitchen paper.

4 Divide the meat mix evenly into 4. Tip the flour on to a plate and roll each egg in it to coat, tapping off any excess. Pat down one-quarter of the meat mix on the work surface to a 12–13 cm (4½–5 inch) disc, using the rest of the flour to keep it from sticking. Cup the disc in your hand and place one of the eggs in the centre. Using both hands, pat, press and ease the meat mix around the egg until it is completely and evenly covered. Seal really well so that there is no join, then pat and roll it into a good shape on the floured surface. Repeat with the rest of the meat mix and cooked eggs.

5 Mix the panko crumbs on a large plate with the remaining chives. Beat the remaining egg on a plate, brush some all over each coated egg (you won't use it all), then roll the eggs in the panko crumbs, patting them on to stick. Lay the eggs on a baking sheet lined with baking parchment and chill for 20–25 minutes (but not overnight). Preheat the oven to 190°C (fan 170°C/375°F/gas mark 5).

6 Heat 2 teaspoons of the remaining oil in the pan you used for the shallot. When quite hot (it is hot enough when a few panko crumbs dropped in sizzle immediately and start to brown), put in 2 of the Scotch eggs and roll in the oil to coat them well. Set the timer for 2 minutes, and fry the eggs, turning often, to brown all over. You are just browning, not fully cooking the eggs at this stage, so don't overcook or the coating may start to split. Transfer to the lined baking sheet and repeat with the remaining eggs and oil, lowering the heat slightly if the pan gets too hot.

7 Bake the Scotch eggs for 12 minutes. Remove, lay them on kitchen paper to drain and leave to cool slightly.

use extra-lean pork mince and medium eggs, rather than large, to reduce fat and swop some of the mince for lentils

•

shallow-fry and bake rather than deep-fry the eggs to reduce fat even more

Creamy mash

Even without lots of butter and full-fat milk, this recipe still makes a soft, creamy mash – the perfect accompaniment to roast or grilled chicken, and many other family favourites.

	Classic	Lighter
Kcals	408	225
Fat	24.7 g	4.1 g
Sat fat	15.2 g	2.4 g
Salt	0.3 g	0.1 g

Per serving 225 kcals

Protein 6.3 g, carbs 40.5 g, fat 4.1 g, sat fat 2.4 g, fibre 3.3 g, sugar 2.3 g, salt 0.1 g

Serves 6

Prep: 10 minutes
Cook: 15 minutes

1.5 kg (3 lb 5 oz) floury potatoes, such as King Edward or Maris Piper, cut into even chunks

125 ml (4 fl oz) semi-skimmed milk

15 g (½ oz) butter

4 tablespoons half-fat crème fraîche

salt and freshly ground black pepper

1 Bring a large saucepan of water to the boil. Add the potatoes and boil for about 15 minutes or until tender. Transfer to a colander and drain well, then return to the pan and set over a very low heat for 2 minutes to dry completely.

2 Heat the milk and butter in a small pan, then pour over the potatoes. Remove the pan from the heat, then mash the potatoes using an electric hand whisk or potato masher. Tip in the crème fraîche and beat with a wooden spoon until smooth and creamy. Season with pepper and a pinch of salt.

Lower the fat and calories by replacing butter with lower-fat milk and half-fat crème fraîche

TIPS FOR MAKING IT LIGHTER

Tips for making it lighter

In choosing and using the recipes in this book, you will have seen that each and every one of them employs at least one way or another of substantially reducing the fat, salt or sugar content of a dish. The methods are quite simple and uncomplicated in many cases, and yet the reduction in calories between one of my lighter dishes and its classic equivalent is often dramatic. As you gain in confidence, you'll be able use the same tricks to adapt classic dishes of your own. Here are some of the best.

TEN WAYS WITH... Meat and fish

- Choose lean cuts of meat for your dishes.

- Trim off excess fat and remove skin from fish and chicken.

- For recipes that call for lardons, use thick slices of ham instead, trimmed of all fat.

- By using poached salmon instead of smoked salmon for a given recipe, you can greatly reduce the salt intake.

- To enhance the flavour of chicken, pork, lamb or fish, marinate in yogurt and spices or oil and herbs before cooking.

- Rub meat with a mix of dried spices prior to cooking. That way, you'll eliminate any need for salt.

- Mix extra vegetables into mince such as grated raw carrot, or use green lentils to add bulk and reduce the amount of mince you need.

- Always use a non-stick pan for frying meat and fish. That way you'll need less oil.

- Better still, if you can grill meat or fish instead of shallow-frying it, you'll need even less oil.

- Instead of serving burgers, fish or chicken with shop-bought sauces, make your own fresh fruit or vegetable salsas.

... Fruit, vegetables and nuts

- Don't bother salting aubergines. It is no longer necessary now that newer varieties are less bitter.

- Boost your fibre intake by leaving the peel on apples and potatoes whenever it is possible.

- Always use soft fruits when in season. They will have the best flavour and be at their sweetest, so you can use less sugar.

- Ring the changes by replacing regular potato with sweet potato or celeriac, or use half and half.

- Cut down on carbohydrates by serving smaller pasta and rice portions, but bump them up with peas, carrots, peppers or courgettes.

- Replace salt entirely using dried porcini mushrooms, fresh herbs, mustard, garlic, Tabasco sauce, crushed dried chillies, lemon or lime. Almost any savoury recipe can use at least one of these great taste boosters.

- Cover the top of cheesy or pasta bakes with halved cherry tomatoes.

- Steam vegetables whenever possible, to minimize nutrient loss.

- Roast rather than fry vegetables to keep fat to a minimum.

- Dry-roast raw nuts and whole spices – it intensifies their flavour.

FIVE WAYS WITH... Dairy and eggs

- By choosing strong-tasting cheeses like Parmesan or extra-mature Cheddar, you'll find you need less of them.

- Infuse milk for savoury sauces with herbs, garlic and shallots, and cut out the salt altogether.

- Replace high-fat creams with half-fat crème fraîche combined with plain yogurt for a creamy topping.

- Use medium-sized eggs, not large, when appropriate.

- Instead of using cream as a base for a pasta sauce, save some of the cooking water.

... Baked goods and desserts

- Replace some of the butter with natural yogurt and rapeseed oil when making pastry or cakes.

- Line baking sheets with baking parchment instead of greasing them with oil or butter.

- When making mousses, replace an egg yolk with whisked egg white for a lower-fat way of increasing volume.

- Use unrefined sugars. For a fudgier taste, combine light or dark muscovado with golden caster sugar.

- Choose good-quality dark chocolate (70% cocoa solids) for its depth of flavour. A little cocoa powder can replace some of the chocolate, but avoid adding too much, as that will give a powdery taste.

Winning substitutes

Rapeseed oil for other oils
Why? It is lower in saturated fat (containing less than half that of olive oil).

Green or brown lentils for mince
Why? It reduces saturated fat dramatically when used half and half. It also increases fibre.

Filo pastry for traditional pastry toppings
Why? It is lower in calories, fat and carbohydrates.

Wholemeal flour for white
Why? It increases fibre and is richer in some nutrients, such as B vitamins. A good ratio is half and half with white (using all wholemeal can make a mixture heavy).

Watercress and rocket for lettuce
Why? Darker leaves tend to be richer in nutrients such as betacarotene.

Calorie countdown

How often do you look at the back of a packet when shopping, to see how many calories a given product has? Calorie counting has become a way of life for many of us and shows that we care about the number of calories we consume, and that, wherever possible, we want to keep within the daily recommended guidelines given on page 10.

The following countdown presents all of the recipes in this book that are below 700 calories per serving, from the highest to the lowest. Whether you are looking for a light lunch, an impressive dessert or a supper to share with the family, the list will help you to make a calorie-conscious choice in no time.

Recipes under 700 calories

649 Kcals: Fish and Chips, page 46
618 Kcals: The Full English Breakfast, page 190
609 Kcals: Paella, page 119

Recipes under 600 calories

527 Kcals: Spaghetti Carbonara, page 94
517 Kcals: Risotto with Squash and Sage, page 40
515 Kcals: Chicken Tikka Masala, page 80
511 Kcals: Cornish Pasties, page 198
503 Kcals: Macaroni Cheese, page 64

Recipes under 500 calories

498 Kcals: Pizza Margherita, page 72
487 Kcals: Thai Green Chicken Curry, page 86
485 Kcals: Chicken Biryani, page 116
475 Kcals: Risotto Primavera, page 104
451 Kcals: Salad Niçoise, page 28
447 Kcals: Lasagne, page 54
430 Kcals: Chicken Caesar Salad, page 24
429 Kcals: Shepherd's Pie, page 70
420 Kcals: Coq au Vin, page 98
413 Kcals: Fish Pie, page 112
405 Kcals: French Onion Soup, page 16

405 Kcals: Nasi Goreng, page 96
405 Kcals: Burgers with Roasted Pepper Salsa, page 74
402 Kcals: Chicken Korma, page 52
402 Kcals: Coronation Chicken, page 32

Recipes under 400 calories

398 Kcals: Fish Chowder, page 36
373 Kcals: Steak and Kidney Pie, page 58
359 Kcals: Treacle Sponge, page 133
353 Kcals: Apple and Blackberry Crumble, page 148
350 Kcals: Beef Wellington, page 108
339 Kcals: Lamb Tagine, page 101
336 Kcals: Coffee and Walnut Cake, page 164
335 Kcals: Fish Chowder, page 36
331 Kcals: Salmon en Croûte, page 90
325 Kcals: Moussaka, page 42
320 Kcals: Chicken Pie, page 66
319 Kcals: Crispy Chicken, page 60
318 Kcals: Fruity Sponge Pudding and Custard, page 130
315 Kcals: New York Cheesecake, page 122
312 Kcals: Bread and Butter Pudding, page 150
309 Kcals: Onion Tart, page 78

Recipes under 300 calories

298 Kcals: Prawn Laksa, page 22
295 Kcals: Spanish Omelette, page 193
280 Kcals: Almond Tart, page 186
272 Kcals: Quiche Lorraine, page 50
271 Kcals: Chocolate Log, page 172
270 Kcals: Coffee Panna Cotta, page 125
269 Kcals: Salmon Teriyaki, page 102
263 Kcals: Victoria Sandwich, page 182
262 Kcals: Chicken Cacciatore, page 83
260 Kcals: Apple Tart, page 143
257 Kcals: Crème Brûlée, page 154
255 Kcals: Mediterranean Fish Stew, page 103
254 Kcals: Greek Salad, page 35
247 Kcals: Treacle Tart, page 167
243 Kcals: Chocolate Tart, page 126
243 Kcals: Lemon Drizzle Cake, page 168
239 Kcals: Fish Cakes, page 49
236 Kcals: Crunchy Granola, page 192
234 Kcals: Chocolate Cup Cakes, page 177
232 Kcals: Potato Dauphinoise, page 206
230 Kcals: Pork Stir-fry, page 57
225 Kcals: Creamy Mash, page 213
223 Kcals: Scotch Eggs, page 210
220 Kcals: Tiramisu, page 134
217 Kcals: Chicken Balti, page 89
217 Kcals: Carrot Cake, page 160
215 Kcals: Potato Salad, page 30
213 Kcals: Creamy Butternut Squash Soup, page 27
213 Kcals: Parmigiana, page 111
206 Kcals: Blueberry Muffins, page 178

Recipes under 200 calories

196 Kcals: Strawberry Ice Cream Milk Shake, page 152
194 Kcals: Banana Bread, page 171
191 Kcals: Chocolate Brownies, page 162
186 Kcals: Prawn Cocktail, page 14
186 Kcals: Lemon Tart, page 138
180 Kcals: Raspberry and Passion Fruit Pavlova, page 153
175 Kcals: Twice-baked Cheese Soufflés, page 18
169 Kcals: Strawberry Fool, page 129
167 Kcals: Chocolate Mousse, page 146
162 Kcals: Semifreddo with Summer Fruits, page 149
161 Kcals: Ratatouille, page 204
160 Kcals: Garlic Bread, page 201
157 Kcals: Salmon Pâté, page 21
157 Kcals: Flapjacks, page 184
148 Kcals: Vanilla Ice Cream, page 144
145 Kcals: Hummus, page 195
141 Kcals: Leek and Potato Soup, page 29
141 Kcals: Roast Vegetables, page 194
130 Kcals: Sticky Gingerbread, page 170
116 Kcals: Oat and Raisin Cookies, page 185
106 Kcals: Peanut Butter Cookies, page 176
99 Kcals: Sausage Rolls, page 196
97 Kcals: Chocolate Chip Cookies, page 180
94 Kcals: Crunchy Coleslaw, page 63
83 Kcals: Creamed Garlicky Spinach, page 205
56 Kcals: Braised Leeks and Peas, page 202
56 Kcals: Pesto, page 208
14 Kcals: Red Onion Marmalade, page 209

Index

I dedicate this book to Elizabeth, Emily and Megan. May it give them as much inspiration as they give to me.

Acknowledgements

A big thank you to all my friends, 'the tasters', who have given their unbiased opinions when sampling these recipes with me. I'm grateful for all of your comments. I am indebted to registered nutritional therapist Kerry Torrens, who provided support and invaluable nutritional advice. She also analysed the new recipes for the book and calculated all the 'health alerts'. Thank you, Kerry – I couldn't have done it without you. Thanks, too, to nutritionists Wendy Doyle and Fiona Hunter, whose expertise I greatly valued while working on the original recipes for *BBC Good Food* magazine. I'd also like to thank the editorial team at *Good Food*, especially the magazine's editor, Gillian Carter, who supported my idea for this book and continues to encourage a healthier way of eating in the magazine. And lastly, many thanks to Octopus Publishing Group for agreeing to publish this book and to the editorial and design team for making it look as good as it does.

Commissioning editor Eleanor Maxfield
Deputy art director Yasia Williams-Leedham
Design Jaz Bahra
Editors Alex Stetter and Katy Denny
Production controller Sarah Kramer

Photo credits

David Munns, apart from the following:
Lara Holmes 37, 155
Gareth Morgans 71
Stuart Ovenden 183
Lis Parsons 67–9, 81, 177, 207
Philip Webb 139 (finished tart), 211
Simon Wheeler 25, 47, 51, 123, 191

Food styling

Angela Nilsen, apart from the following:
Lizzie Harris 37, 211
Jane Hornby 139 (finished tart), 183
Jennifer Joyce 155
Lucy O'Reilly 61